HOW TO OVERCOME SHAME

Dr. Maxwell Shimba

Shimba Publishing LLC

TABLE OF CONTENTS

INTRODUCTION

Many people around the world, both Christians and non-Christians, are burdened by the weight of shame. For some, this shame stems from their own sinful actions. Others carry shame because it has been unjustly imposed on them by those who have condemned them. Still, others have inherited a cycle of shameful behavior or feelings passed down from their parents.

Shame is a powerful emotion that can keep you tethered to the past, preventing you from rising to fulfill the destiny God has planned for you. The aim of this book is to guide you in overcoming the shame that has held you, your loved ones, or those you minister to, in bondage.

Shame is one of the most destructive forces in the world, which is why so many today are weighed down by it. There are three primary reasons why people carry such heavy burdens of shame:

1. Some feel ashamed because of their own sinful conduct.

2. Some bear shame that has been imposed upon them by others.

3. Others have inherited a cycle of shameful behavior from previous generations.

Addressing shame is crucial because:

1. It will allow you to break free from the emotional chains that keep you bound to the past.

2. It will empower you to rise up and fulfill your God-given destiny.

3. It will liberate you from bondage, enabling you to focus on the future.

The purpose of this book is to help you overcome the shame that has bound you, your loved ones, or those to whom you minister. Whether it's the shame of divorce, abortion, sexual abuse, abandonment, or any other sinful act committed by you or against you, you no longer need to carry it.

The key to being set free, not just from sin but also from the bondage of shame, is the truth of God's Word. "You shall know the truth, and the truth shall set you free."

DR. MAXWELL SHIMBA

CHAPTER 01

What is Shame according to the Bible?

Shame, as described in the Bible, is deeply intertwined with the human experience of sin and the resulting separation from God. According to Baker's Evangelical Dictionary of Biblical Theology, shame is a consequence of sin, representing a relational breach rather than just a legal or moral failing. While guilt is judicial, addressing the violation of laws or commandments, shame is more relational, reflecting the deep sense of dishonor and disgrace that comes from realizing one's actions have broken the covenant with God.

The Bible first introduces the concept of shame in the story of Adam and Eve in Genesis. After they disobeyed God's command by eating from the Tree of Knowledge of Good and Evil, they immediately felt shame, symbolized by their sudden awareness of their nakedness and their attempt to cover themselves. This moment marked the beginning of humanity's struggle with shame as a direct result of sin.

Throughout Scripture, shame is often depicted as both a consequence of sin and a tool of punishment for disobedience. In the Old Testament, prophets like Jeremiah speak of the shame that will fall upon Israel due to their idolatry and unfaithfulness to God. Similarly, in the New Testament, Jesus warns of the shame that will come upon those who deny Him before others.

However, the Bible also offers a message of hope and redemption for those burdened by shame. God promises, especially in the book of Isaiah, to remove the shame of His people and restore their honor. The New Testament reinforces this message, with the apostle Paul proclaiming that in Christ, there is no shame—believers are made equal and whole in the eyes of God.

Shame can exert a powerful influence over our lives, often dictating our actions, thoughts, and self-perception. It can become a controlling force, but the Bible teaches that it doesn't have to be this way. Through God's grace, there is a path to freedom from shame—a way to rewrite our stories and live without the burden of disgrace.

While shame is closely related to guilt, it is important to distinguish the two. Shame is the emotional and relational response to guilt and wrongdoing. Admitting and confronting our shame is a crucial step towards change and spiritual growth. Through Christ, we are offered a way to overcome shame and embrace the identity and worth that God has given us.

Guilt means "debt" and it is essentially an emotion resulting from the transgression of an accepted standard by a definite, voluntary act.

It is a feeling of deserving blame from some breach of conduct, or from a sense of inadequacy.

The difference between guilt and shame according to Apostle Paul; He illustrated when he said, "For the good that I will to do, I do not do; but the evil I will not to do, that I: That is guilt emanating from doing. Then Paul agonizes, "Oh wretched man that I am! Who will deliver me from this body of death?" This is the cry of a tormented soul experiencing the shame of being.

In Romans 7:24, "What a wretched man I am! Who will rescue me from this body that is subject to death?" the ancient Greek word "wretched" is more literally, "wretched through the exhaustion of hard labor." Paul was completely worn out and desolate because of his unsuccessful efforts to please God under the principle of Law.

Shame drives you on a hunting expedition into your past, scrutinizing everything you have done wrong and building a case against you like an aggressive prosecutor in a court of law. "A vague, undefined heaviness that presses on our spirit, dampens our gratitude for the goodness of life, and slackens the free flow of joy. Shame...seeps into and discolors all our other feelings, primarily about ourselves, but about almost everyone and everything else in our life as well."

Shame is especially difficult, if not toxic, for children because it is an emotion that is concealed, especially by victims of aggression or abuse.

In contrast to shame, what is the purpose of guilt?

While shame and guilt are often used interchangeably, they are distinct emotional experiences with different purposes.

Guilt is the feeling of remorse or regret that arises when we believe we have violated a moral or ethical standard, or have harmed someone else. Unlike shame, which is focused on the self and can be accompanied by feelings of worthlessness or inadequacy, guilt is focused on the behavior or action and can be a motivating force for change or restitution.

The purpose of guilt is to promote moral behavior and social harmony by encouraging individuals to take responsibility for their actions and make amends when necessary. By feeling guilty, we acknowledge that we have done something wrong and are more likely to take steps to correct our behavior, apologize to those we have harmed, and make reparations if possible.

Guilt can also have social benefits by signaling to others that we are trustworthy and dependable members of a community. When we feel guilty for our actions, we are more likely to be perceived as sincere and trustworthy by others, which can help to maintain social bonds and promote cooperation and mutual support.

Overall, while guilt can be an uncomfortable emotion, it serves an important purpose in promoting moral behavior and social cohesion.

Furthermore, guilt leads to godly sorrow which results in Paul explaining that the Old Testament law was designed for this purpose: 19 Now we know that whatever the law says, it says to those who are under the law, so that every mouth may be silenced and the whole world held accountable to God. 20 Therefore no one will be declared righteous in God's sight by the works of the law; rather, through the law we become conscious of our sin. Romans 3:19-20

"Sorrow of the World"

Worldly sorrow centers on ourselves. It's the guilt we feel when we're caught, when others might think less of us, or when our carefully crafted image is tarnished. This type of sorrow is entirely focused on our own emotions and how we are perceived by others.

In contrast, godly sorrow shifts the focus away from our own feelings and toward God. It is the deep sorrow we feel when we recognize how our actions have offended God. This kind of sorrow drives us to seek forgiveness and to make things right with God, leading us to true repentance and a commitment to change, with no regrets.

Shame sets two distinct processes in motion:

1. Negative Shame: When shame is denied, it can turn into anger. Anger often serves as a socially acceptable outlet, but beneath it lies a range of hidden emotions—shame, feelings of inadequacy, low self-esteem, and a sense of being unloved or unlovable.

2. Positive Guilt: When guilt is acknowledged and confessed, it can lead to positive change.

Shame hinders intimacy with God because it makes us feel unworthy. Shame is closely tied to the loss of respect from others and the erosion of self-respect. This is especially true when we are hiding a secret sin, such as pornography. The shame over this hidden sin creates a wall between us and God, preventing us from experiencing true intimacy with Him.

Choosing to live in secret sin ultimately traps us in a cycle of fear and separation—fear of being discovered by others and separation from God. This choice can lead to significant physical, emotional, and psychological consequences. To remain in shame over secret sin is to accept a life of defeat and bondage, distanced from God.

Shame can torment you in two ways:

1. Internally: Through the constant guilt and unease in your conscience.

2. Externally: Through the judgment and condemnation from others.

The origins of shame are complex and likely date back to before recorded history. Some theories suggest that shame may have developed as a mechanism to regulate social behavior and maintain order within early human communities. These societies were built on cooperation and interdependence, so when someone violated social norms or acted selfishly, they risked being ostracized or expelled from the group. This social rejection would have triggered feelings of shame, serving as a powerful motivator to conform to social norms and ensure group harmony.

Some scholars suggest that shame is closely linked to the development of self-awareness and the recognition of our own limitations and imperfections. As humans evolved greater cognitive abilities and self-consciousness, they became increasingly aware of their flaws and weaknesses, which led to feelings of shame when they fell short of their own or others' expectations.

The origins of shame are likely complex and multifaceted, and they continue to be a subject of study for psychologists, anthropologists, and other researchers.

Shame first emerged in the context of original sin. Humanity's initial transgression arose from a desire to be something other than what God created us to be—to surpass our human limitations. Adam and Eve's shame-free existence was short-lived. After eating the forbidden fruit, they covered themselves with fig leaves, not wanting to be seen. They felt unworthy and embarrassed because their disobedience to God's commands brought shame into their lives.

Sin shattered three fundamental human relationships:
1. Man's relationship with God:
   - To rebuild our relationship with God:
      1. We must abandon every excuse and justification.
      2. We must let go of our pride and stop hiding from God, thinking He is unaware of our actions.
      3. We must be convinced that God's way is better than our own.
2. Man's relationship with himself.
3. Man's relationship with others.

To restore these broken relationships, we must address the roots of shame and the impact of sin:
1. Man's Relationship with God:
   - Rebuilding our connection with God requires humility and honesty. We must stop hiding behind excuses and acknowledge that God knows our hearts and actions. Recognizing that God's wisdom and guidance surpass our own is essential in restoring this relationship.
2. Man's Relationship with Himself:
   - Sin not only distorts our relationship with God but also disrupts our inner peace and self-understanding. Shame causes us to view ourselves through a lens of inadequacy and unworthiness. To heal this relationship, we must embrace the

truth of our identity in God, understanding that we are created in His image and are loved unconditionally. This self-awareness helps us overcome the destructive power of shame.

3. Man's Relationship with Others:

- Sin also fractures our connections with other people. Shame can lead to isolation, defensiveness, and a breakdown in communication. Restoring these relationships involves practicing forgiveness, seeking reconciliation, and fostering empathy. It's about breaking down the walls that shame builds between us and others, allowing for genuine and loving connections to flourish.

In summary, shame has deep and ancient roots, but it is not insurmountable. By addressing the damage caused by sin and shame in our relationships with God, ourselves, and others, we can begin to experience true healing and restoration. It requires a commitment to humility, self-awareness, and love—foundations that will help us rebuild and strengthen these vital connections.

CHAPTER 02

The Generational Shame

What is Generational Shame?

Generational shame is a deep-seated form of shame that traces its roots back to the Garden of Eden, continuing to affect humanity through the ages like an uncontrolled aircraft caught in a powerful wind shear. This shame spirals through time, generating countless reactions based on shame, triggered by words, sounds, feelings, and even tastes and smells.

When trapped in generational shame, it may feel nearly impossible to imagine a life free from it. You might experience an overwhelming sense of lack or worthlessness, leading to isolation, depression, or the tendency to blame others. The pain and difficulty of this experience can be so intense that you may feel desperate to escape it by any means possible.

In a broader sense, generational shame refers to the shame passed down through families or cultural groups over multiple generations. This can stem from past events or actions, such as historical traumas, cultural injustices, or family secrets, and it can have a profound impact on the identity and well-being of individuals and communities.

For example, generational shame may be felt by descendants of groups who have endured colonization, slavery, genocide, or other forms of systemic oppression. The trauma and stigma associated with these events can be inherited, leading to feelings of shame, guilt, and a sense of cultural or ancestral inferiority that persists through generations.

Generational Shame and Its Consequences

Generational shame can also arise from family secrets or unresolved traumas that are kept hidden or never openly discussed. For instance, when a family history of addiction, mental illness, or abuse is concealed or denied, it can lead to deep feelings of shame and isolation for those affected.

The impact of generational shame can be profound, contributing to negative mental and physical health outcomes, a sense of disconnection from one's cultural roots or identity, and difficulties in forming and maintaining healthy relationships. Healing from generational shame often requires confronting and processing the past, cultivating a sense of cultural pride and connection, and fostering supportive relationships within the community.

Shame manifests in various ways, including:

1. Paranoia: Shame whispers, "They don't like you. You don't belong. They think you're not good enough."

2. Personalization: People who carry shame often internalize everything. This behavior starts early in life; for example, as children, seeing another child reading a more

advanced book while we are still reading a simpler one can make us feel ashamed. And so, the cycle of shame begins.

3. Generalization: Shame distorts your thinking, making isolated incidents feel like a reflection of your entire self-worth.

4. Rationalization: A person burdened by shame frequently rationalizes their behavior to avoid confronting their feelings of inadequacy.

5. Repression: Another way people cope with shame is by repressing or denying the events that caused it.

6. Condemnation: Shame's voice repeats in your mind like a stuck record, continuously reinforcing negative self-perceptions. This can lead to a situation where you feel ashamed of feeling shame itself.

7. Helplessness: Shame convinces you that you are a victim of circumstances, stripping away your sense of agency and control.

8. A Shame-Based Conscience: Some people try to navigate shame by letting their conscience guide them, adhering to internal morals, principles, and standards. However, if your internal voice constantly says, "You are not good enough," it's crucial to recognize that this voice does not represent your true self—it is the voice of the Accuser, the Father of Lies.

To break free from the cycle of shame, it is essential to confront and challenge these effects, recognizing that the internal and external voices perpetuating feelings of worthlessness are not the truth of who you are.

Do Shame-Based People Magnify Their Flaws?

It's worth considering whether, as parents, we might unintentionally contribute to this by frequently pointing out our children's flaws. Our intention may be to help them grow into successful, productive members of society, believing that the best way to achieve this is by correcting every bad habit from the start. However, without realizing it, we may become overly controlling and critical, not allowing our children the space to make their own choices and experience the natural consequences of their actions.

What is the Difference Between Condemnation and the Conviction of the Holy Spirit?

Condemnation and the conviction of the Holy Spirit are distinct concepts in Christian theology.

Condemnation refers to God's judgment against sin, resulting in punishment or eternal separation from God. It is the consequence of willfully rejecting God's offer of salvation through faith in Jesus Christ. Condemnation is a final verdict, declaring a person guilty of sin and deserving of punishment.

The conviction of the Holy Spirit, on the other hand, is the inner prompting and guidance from the Holy Spirit that leads a person to recognize their sin and turn to God for forgiveness and salvation. This conviction is not intended to bring shame or condemnation but to inspire repentance and restoration. The Holy Spirit convicts individuals of sin to lead them to salvation, not to condemn them.

In summary, condemnation is God's final judgment against sin, while the conviction of the Holy Spirit is the inner prompting that leads to repentance and salvation. Conviction is specific, focusing on a particular sin and eliciting godly sorrow, which leads to confession and repentance. Condemnation, in contrast, is generalized and declares a person guilty and hopeless without remedy. However, when our identity is centered in Christ—knowing both who we are in Christ and who He is in us—we can shed the dark shroud of shame and rise in radiance. We may experience feelings of shame, but in Jesus, shame no longer has power over us.

Summary of Conscience in the Following Scriptures:
- 1 Corinthians 8:12: A weak conscience.
- Titus 1:15: A defiled conscience.

- 1 Timothy 4:2: A seared conscience, as if branded with a hot iron.

Why is it Dangerous to Let Your Conscience Be Your Guide?

Relying solely on one's conscience as a guide can be dangerous for several reasons:

1. Subjectivity: Our conscience is shaped by our personal experiences, beliefs, and biases, and may not always be reliable or accurate in guiding our behavior. For instance, if someone grows up in a culture that values aggression and violence, their conscience might lead them to act in harmful ways, even if they believe they are acting morally.

2. External Influences: Our conscience can be swayed by external factors such as peer pressure or societal norms, which may cause us to act against our values or beliefs. In some cases, people may even use their conscience to justify harmful or immoral actions, such as discrimination or violence against certain groups.

3. Moral Relativism: Depending solely on our conscience can lead to moral relativism, where there is no objective standard of right and wrong. Without an external moral framework, individuals may justify their actions based on their subjective moral code, leading to conflicting interpretations of what is right or wrong.

Overall, while our conscience can be a useful tool for guiding our behavior, it should not be relied upon as the sole source of moral guidance. It's important to also consider external moral frameworks, such as ethical principles or religious teachings, and to seek guidance and input from others to ensure that our actions align with our values and serve the best interests of ourselves and others.

Conscience and Its True Guide

Our conscience is often shaped by our environment and experiences rather than being guided by the Holy Spirit.

Nowhere in Scripture does the Bible suggest, "Let your conscience be your guide" or "Be true to your own heart." The problem with this kind of advice is that our hearts, minds, and consciences are just as fallen and prone to error as our emotions.

The Only Remedy for a Shameful Conscience

According to Christian theology, the only true remedy for a shameful conscience is forgiveness through faith in Jesus Christ. The Bible teaches that all humans have sinned and fall short of the glory of God, and that the penalty for sin is death (Romans 3:23, 6:23). However, the good news of the gospel is that through faith in Jesus Christ, we can receive forgiveness and salvation, cleansing our conscience from guilt and shame. This is grounded in the belief that Jesus Christ died on the cross as a sacrifice for sin, and through His death and resurrection, believers are offered new life (1 Peter 2:24, Romans 10:9).

In addition to seeking forgiveness through faith in Jesus Christ, addressing a shameful conscience may also involve pursuing healing and restoration through counseling, support groups, or other forms of therapy. This process often includes identifying and addressing underlying issues such as trauma, negative self-talk, or distorted beliefs about self-worth and identity.

Shame is like a heavy weight that pulls you down whenever you try to rise toward your God-given destiny. No matter what has caused your shame—whether it's filing for bankruptcy, struggling with an addiction, losing your job due to a mistake, or anything else—by grace through faith in Jesus Christ, you can overcome shame and fulfill His purposes for your life.

Why Are Shame-Based Reactions Initiated?

Shame-based reactions occur when an individual perceives a threat to their sense of self-worth, competence, or identity. These threats can be either real or perceived and may stem from external sources, such as criticism, rejection, or social exclusion, or internal sources, such as self-doubt, self-criticism, or internalized negative beliefs.

Shame-based reactions are often characterized by feelings of embarrassment, inadequacy, or worthlessness, accompanied by physical symptoms like blushing, sweating, or an increased heart rate. In response to these feelings, individuals may withdraw from social situations, avoid tasks or challenges, or engage in self-destructive behaviors such as substance abuse or self-harm.

These reactions can be particularly harmful because they often lead to a cycle of self-perpetuating negative thoughts and behaviors. For example, if someone feels ashamed of a mistake, they may avoid taking risks or trying new things in the future, leading to a lack of personal growth and development.

It's important to recognize that shame-based reactions are not always rational or proportional to the situation at hand. They may be influenced by past experiences, cultural beliefs, or other factors. Addressing these reactions typically involves identifying the underlying beliefs and triggers, challenging negative self-talk, and developing a more compassionate and self-affirming perspective.

Common Shame-Based Reactions:

1. Scapegoating: This concept originates from an Old Testament practice involving a blood sacrifice for sin.

2. Perfectionism: Shame often drives people to prove their worth by striving for perfection.

3. Self-Punishment: Some individuals resort to self-harm or other forms of punishment to atone for their shame.

4. Defensiveness: People who are shame-based often interpret criticism of their actions as a judgment of their character.

5. Patronizing: This is a subtle way of deflecting shame onto others by offering support and encouragement with a condescending attitude.

6. Controlling: A shame-based person may try to control others' thoughts, feelings, and actions to prevent being shamed again.

7. Arrogance and Self-Righteousness: Arrogance is often a psychological cover for shame, with the person hiding their true self from others and themselves.

8. Addictions: Psychologist John Bradshaw suggests that shame is the core and fuel for all addictive behavior.

9. Aggression: A shame-based person may not value themselves, leading to disrespect for others, anger, and potentially violent or criminal behavior if combined with power.

10. Alienation and Dissociation: Sometimes, a shame-based person will isolate themselves to avoid further shame.

Despite the overwhelming nature of shame, there is hope. Scripture promises that when we turn to God, He can transform our shame into something beautiful—bringing joy and peace at last.

The Positive Side of Mistakes

Mistakes, though often frustrating or embarrassing, can offer several positive benefits:

1. Learning: Mistakes provide valuable learning opportunities. Reflecting on what went wrong and how to do things differently in the future helps improve skills and knowledge, preventing the same mistake from being repeated.

2. Resilience: Experiencing failure or setbacks helps build resilience and adaptability, enabling us to bounce back and persevere through challenges.

3. Creativity: Mistakes can inspire creativity and innovation, forcing us to think outside the box and develop new solutions to problems.

4. Humility: Mistakes teach humility and foster empathy and compassion for others who face their own challenges.

While mistakes can be difficult in the moment, they are also opportunities for growth and development. Rather than avoiding mistakes at all costs, we can embrace them as part of the learning process and use them to our advantage.

Mistakes offer feedback—every error tells us what needs to be corrected. However, if you become too preoccupied with defending yourself against the inner critical voices, you may miss the opportunity to learn from the mistake and grow.

Embracing Mistake-Driven Learning

I like to call this approach "mistake-driven learning." The key is to learn from our mistakes, then move on and leave them behind. The Apostle Paul captured this mindset perfectly in Philippians 3:13: "But one thing I do: Forgetting what is behind and straining toward what is ahead."

The Self-Righteousness of the Pharisees and Sadducees

The Pharisees and Sadducees were two influential religious groups in Jewish society during New Testament times, both of which exemplified self-righteousness in their religious practices.

The Pharisees were known for their meticulous observance of the law and their focus on external displays of piety. They believed that salvation was achieved through strict adherence to the law, rituals, and traditions. However, their commitment to these practices often led them to judge and look down on those who did not meet their rigorous standards. They were particularly critical of Jesus for associating with sinners and for not conforming to their interpretations of the law.

The Sadducees, in contrast, were primarily concerned with temple worship and the priestly duties that accompanied it. They did not believe in the resurrection or the afterlife and were more focused on maintaining their social and political power. Like the Pharisees, they viewed themselves as morally superior to others and frequently clashed with Jesus and His teachings.

Both groups demonstrated self-righteousness by emphasizing outward displays of piety and adopting a judgmental attitude toward those who did not conform to their standards. Their concern was more with maintaining their status and power than with genuinely serving God and others. Jesus, on the other hand, emphasized humility, compassion, and love, and He often rebuked the self-righteousness of the religious leaders of His day (Matthew 23:1-12).

These leaders gave, prayed, and fasted to be seen by others, demanding that everyone else adhere to their stringent and oppressive standards.

However, it's important to acknowledge the dedication of the Pharisees:

1. To be a Pharisee, one had to memorize the first five books of the Bible.

2. They attended the synagogue whenever it was open.

3. They fasted and prayed regularly.

4. They tithed with great diligence.

5. They believed in the one true God.

Many people we counsel for shame might say they attend church regularly, give offerings every Sunday, and have memorized some Bible verses. Yet, like the Pharisee Nicodemus in John 3, they need to be truly born again—born of the Spirit, born spiritually. As Jesus said in John 3:5, "Very truly I tell you, no one can enter the kingdom of God unless they are born of water and the Spirit."

The Connection Between Shame and Addictive Behavior

Shame can be a powerful driving force behind addictive behaviors. When individuals experience deep feelings of shame, they may turn to substances or behaviors as a way to numb or escape the pain associated with their shame. This can create a vicious cycle where the behavior or substance temporarily alleviates the feelings of shame, but ultimately reinforces the very shame they are trying to avoid.

How Does Shame Relate to Addictive Behavior?

1. Escape and Numbing: People who struggle with shame often use addictive behaviors as a means of escape. Whether it's alcohol, drugs, gambling, or any other form of addiction, these behaviors provide a temporary escape from the intense emotions of shame. However, the relief is short-lived, and the shame usually returns stronger than before, leading to further reliance on the addictive behavior.

2. Self-Punishment: Shame can also drive individuals to punish themselves through addictive behaviors. This self-destructive pattern is a way of coping with the intense feelings of unworthiness and self-loathing that often accompany shame. The addiction becomes a form of self-punishment, reinforcing the negative self-image and deepening the cycle of shame and addiction.

3. Isolation and Secrecy: Shame often leads to isolation, as individuals may hide their struggles out of fear of judgment or rejection. This secrecy can intensify addictive behaviors, as the person feels increasingly alone and trapped in their addiction. The lack of connection and support makes it harder to break free from the cycle of addiction.

4. Reinforcement of Negative Beliefs: Addictive behaviors often reinforce the negative beliefs that underlie shame. For example, if someone believes they are unworthy or incapable of change, the cycle of addiction can confirm

these beliefs, making it even harder to seek help or believe in the possibility of recovery.

Breaking the Cycle: Addressing Shame in Addiction Recovery

Addressing the root causes of shame is essential in breaking the cycle of addiction. This often involves:

- Acknowledging and Confronting Shame: The first step is to bring the hidden shame into the light, acknowledging its presence and its impact on one's life. This can be done through therapy, support groups, or talking with a trusted individual.

- Developing Self-Compassion: Learning to treat oneself with kindness and understanding is crucial in overcoming shame. Self-compassion involves recognizing that everyone makes mistakes and that these mistakes do not define one's worth.

- Building Healthy Connections: Overcoming shame often requires building connections with others who can provide support, understanding, and acceptance. Healthy relationships can help to counteract the isolation that shame creates.

- Focusing on Spiritual Renewal: For many, faith and spiritual practices play a significant role in healing from shame. Understanding one's identity in Christ and the forgiveness offered through His sacrifice can be transformative in breaking free from both shame and addiction.

- Establishing New Patterns: Recovery involves replacing addictive behaviors with healthier coping mechanisms and new, positive patterns of behavior. This might include developing hobbies, engaging in regular physical activity, or pursuing meaningful goals.

Shame and addiction are deeply intertwined, but through awareness, support, and a commitment to change, it is possible to break free from their grip and move towards healing and wholeness.

The Role of Shame in Addictive Behavior

Shame is often a significant factor in driving addictive behavior, as it can push individuals to seek substances or engage in behaviors that offer temporary relief from feelings of inadequacy or unworthiness.

Shame is a deeply painful emotion that arises when individuals believe they have violated social norms or moral values or when they see themselves as inherently flawed or unworthy. This can lead to a negative self-image and feelings of self-disgust, which are difficult to endure. In an effort to escape these overwhelming emotions, individuals may turn to substances or compulsive behaviors that provide a temporary sense of relief or distraction.

For instance, someone struggling with addiction might use drugs or alcohol to numb their emotions and avoid confronting feelings of shame and self-doubt. Others may engage in compulsive behaviors such as gambling, overeating, or sexual activity as a way to distract themselves from their negative thoughts and emotions.

However, while these behaviors may offer temporary relief, they often create a cycle of shame and guilt that perpetuates the addiction. As the addiction deepens, individuals may engage in increasingly risky or harmful behaviors, leading to even more shame and self-blame. This creates a vicious cycle in which shame drives the addiction, and the addiction, in turn, fuels further shame.

Breaking this cycle requires addressing the underlying feelings of shame and inadequacy that may be driving the addictive behavior. This might involve seeking therapy, participating in support groups, or pursuing other forms of treatment that target the root causes of the addiction and help individuals develop healthy coping mechanisms for dealing with difficult emotions.

Addiction, whether it involves substances or compulsive activities (like work, shopping, or gambling), is often an attempt to form an intimate relationship. Each addictive act, however, leads to life-damaging consequences, which in turn generate more shame. This new shame then fuels the cycle of addiction.

The pain of shame is often so unbearable that some people turn to drugs, alcohol, or other addictive behaviors as a way to relieve it. Paradoxically, shame also keeps them trapped in the cycle. The shame of being an addict continuously feeds back into a perpetuating negative cycle, distancing them from others and preventing them from making truthful observations about their behavior and the underlying issues driving it.

Five Manifestations of Shame:

1. Inherited Shame: This is the shame that results from the basic sin nature all humans inherit at birth due to the original transgression of humanity in the Garden of Eden.

2. Individual Shame: This form of shame arises from the sins that one personally commits.

3. Incessant Shame: This refers to the continuous cycle of shame that passes from generation to generation. If shame is not successfully addressed, it is passed on to one's children, who then pass it on to the next generation.

4. Imposed Shame: This type of shame is inflicted by others who belittle or demean you, telling you that you are stupid or not good enough.

5. Institutional Shame: This form of shame comes from societal institutions. You might be shamed because of the color of your skin, your family background, or the city or nation in which you live.

Shame can be a prison of its own making, and recognizing it, along with realizing that one does not deserve to be trapped in that prison, can be difficult. As faith-based counselors, our role is to uncover the lies that cause people to live in shame and replace those lies with the truth found in God's Word.

CHAPTER 03

Inherited Shame

Inherited shame refers to the idea that shame can be passed down from one generation to the next, often through family and cultural beliefs and values.

For example, if a family has a history of shame related to a particular behavior or circumstance, such as addiction or mental illness, this shame can be internalized by future generations, even if they have not personally experienced the same behavior or circumstance. The shame may be perpetuated through family dynamics, cultural expectations, or other societal pressures, and can have a profound impact on an individual's sense of self-worth and identity.

Inherited shame can also be related to broader cultural or societal beliefs and values, such as shame related to race, ethnicity, or sexual orientation. In some cultures, shame may be used as a means of control or punishment, and can be passed down from one generation to the next.

Breaking the cycle of inherited shame can be a complex and challenging process, requiring individuals to confront and challenge deeply ingrained beliefs and cultural norms. Therapy, support groups, and other forms of treatment can be helpful in addressing inherited shame and learning to develop a more positive sense of self-worth and identity. Additionally, raising awareness and promoting acceptance and understanding of diverse experiences and identities can help to break down the barriers created by inherited shame and promote healing and growth.

How does shame erect a barrier between you and God?

Shame can erect a barrier between an individual and God in several ways:

1. Feeling unworthy: When an individual experiences shame, they may feel that they are inherently flawed or unworthy of God's love and acceptance. This can lead to a sense of spiritual disconnection and a belief that they are not deserving of a relationship with God.

2. Hiding from God: Shame can also lead individuals to hide from God, either by avoiding prayer, religious practices, or other forms of spiritual connection. They may feel that they are not good enough to approach God or that God would not want to be associated with someone who has made mistakes or has flaws.

3. Negative self-talk: Shame can also lead to negative self-talk and self-criticism, which can create a mental barrier between an individual and God. They may believe that they are not worthy of forgiveness or redemption and that their mistakes or shortcomings make them unlovable in the eyes of God.

4. Loss of hope: Finally, shame can lead to a loss of hope and a sense of spiritual despair. Individuals may feel that they have strayed too far from God or that their mistakes are too great to be forgiven. This can create a sense of hopelessness and a belief that there is no way to repair the relationship with God.

In order to overcome these barriers and reconnect with God, it is important for individuals to recognize that shame is a normal emotion and that they are not alone in their struggles. Seeking spiritual guidance, practicing self-compassion, and engaging in acts of service and kindness can all help to rebuild a sense of connection with God and overcome the barriers created by shame.

By erecting a spiritual partition between you and God through the shackles of your past.

Actually, shame could be considered another term for unbelief in God's love for you in Christ. Shame creates a barrier that keeps love from getting through – not only God's love but often, also, anyone else's love.

Inherited Shame: The First Level of Shame

The first level of shame is known as inherited shame. This type of shame stems from the basic sin nature that all humans receive at birth due to the original sin committed by humanity in the Garden of Eden. Before this original sin, Adam and Eve were sinless and knew no shame.

What is inherited shame? Inherited shame results from the original sin and the basic sin nature that we all inherit at birth.

The Ripple Effect of Shame

Shame has a ripple effect, drawing others into its grasp. In the case of Eve, her shame led Adam to yield to the same temptation, illustrating how shame spreads. When we sin, we create barriers not only between ourselves and God but also between ourselves and others—our spouse, children, friends, and co-workers. Instead of simply saying, "I'm sorry," and asking for forgiveness, we often choose to hide.

Why was Adam afraid when God came to meet with him and Eve? Adam was afraid because he was naked and ashamed.

Adam's shame led to several consequences:

1. Alienation: Adam felt separated from God and others.

2. Withdrawal: He retreated and hid from God.

3. Cover-Up: Adam attempted to hide his shame with fig leaves, an outward symbol of the barrier created by sin.

Before they sinned, Adam and Eve were not embarrassed by their nakedness. Their shame and awkwardness after sinning pointed to the barrier that their disobedience had built between them and God.

How Shame Was Passed to Succeeding Generations

Shame has been passed down through generations by the inheritance of the basic sin nature, which drives us into a cycle of sin and shame. The original transgression in the Garden of Eden created a sinful nature that was transmitted to all succeeding generations, leading to the sad reality that "all have sinned and fall short of the glory of God" (Romans 3:23).

Can you imagine the shame and regret Adam and Eve must have felt after their sin? They marred the perfect creation that God had made. Adam and Eve lived in a perfect world, with perfect minds and bodies, and enjoyed perfect fellowship with God. When they chose to sin against God, all of creation was subjected to sin's effects, including disease, decay, death, and eternal separation from God. Every human being born afterward inherited this sin nature, which is a natural inclination to sin.

The Flesh or the Old Man

When we refer to the "flesh" or the "old man," we are talking about the inherited shame that comes with our basic sin nature, which all of us must confront and overcome.

The Inherited Sin Nature and Its Consequences

What does the inherited sin nature give rise to? It gives birth to the works of the flesh, as clearly outlined in Galatians 5:19-21. The Scripture lists the works of the flesh as follows:

"Now the works of the flesh are evident: sexual immorality, impurity, sensuality, idolatry, sorcery, enmity, strife, jealousy, fits of anger, rivalries, dissensions, divisions, envy, drunkenness, orgies, and things like these."

However, the works of the flesh aren't always as overt as those listed above. They can also manifest subtly within Christian ministries, where individuals may seek popularity or self-worth under the guise of serving Christ. This was the case with Diotrephes, who was rebuked for such behavior in 3 John 1:9. Trying to please God from a place of selfish motivation often leads to unhealthy competition, slander, bitterness, and ultimately, burnout (Galatians 1:10).

In Romans 7, the Apostle Paul provides a candid summary of his own struggle with the flesh. This chapter is especially comforting to those who are burdened by the awareness of their indwelling sin, caught in spiritual battles known only to themselves and God, the Searcher of Hearts.

Romans 8 shifts the focus to life through the Spirit. Here, Paul declares that those who live in Christ Jesus are free from condemnation, liberated from the law of sin and death. He explains that sharing in Christ's sufferings means we will also share in His glory. The present sufferings we endure because we are united with Christ are insignificant compared to the glory that is to come. Those who belong to Christ understand that the pains of this world are temporary, and something far greater awaits.

While we are sinners, we are now justified. Though we have a shameful past, we look forward to a better future. Where we once walked in foolishness and rebellion, we now walk in the newness of life (Titus 3:3–7; Romans 6:4). God has forgiven the sins that burden us with shame and regret, and we are free to move forward.

Scripture on Shame and Redemption

- Isaiah 50:7: "But the Lord God helps me; therefore, I have not been disgraced; therefore, I have set my face like a flint, and I know that I shall not be put to shame."

- Isaiah 61:7: "Instead of your shame, there shall be a double portion; instead of dishonor, they shall rejoice in their lot; therefore, in their land, they shall possess a double portion; they shall have everlasting joy."

- 1 John 1:9: "If we confess our sins, he is faithful and just to forgive us our sins and to cleanse us from all unrighteousness."

- Psalm 34:4-5: "I sought the Lord, and he answered me and delivered me from all my fears. Those who look to him are radiant, and their faces shall never be ashamed."

- Romans 10:11: "For the Scripture says, 'Everyone who believes in him will not be put to shame.'"

- Psalm 31:17: "O Lord, let me not be put to shame, for I call upon you; let the wicked be put to shame; let them go silently to Sheol."

- Mark 8:38: "For whoever is ashamed of me and of my words in this adulterous and sinful generation, of him will the Son of Man also be ashamed when he comes in the glory of his Father with the holy angels."

- Romans 8:1: "There is therefore now no condemnation for those who are in Christ Jesus."

- Isaiah 54:4: "Fear not, for you will not be ashamed; be not confounded, for you will not be disgraced; for you will forget the shame of your youth, and the reproach of your widowhood you will remember no more."

- Psalm 3:3: "But you, O Lord, are a shield about me, my glory, and the lifter of my head."

- Luke 9:26: "For whoever is ashamed of me and of my words, of him will the Son of Man be ashamed when he comes in his glory and the glory of the Father and of the holy angels."

- Genesis 2:25: "And the man and his wife were both naked and were not ashamed."

- Proverbs 11:2: "When pride comes, then comes disgrace, but with the humble is wisdom."

- Psalm 37:18-19: "The Lord knows the days of the blameless, and their heritage will remain forever; they are not put to shame in evil times; in the days of famine, they have abundance."

- Romans 1:16: "For I am not ashamed of the gospel, for it is the power of God for salvation to everyone who believes, to the Jew first and also to the Greek."

- Nahum 1:7: "The Lord is good, a stronghold in the day of trouble; he knows those who take refuge in him."

- 1 John 2:28: "And now, little children, abide in him, so that when he appears we may have confidence and not shrink from him in shame at his coming."

- Daniel 12:2: "And many of those who sleep in the dust of the earth shall awake, some to everlasting life, and some to shame and everlasting contempt."

- Psalm 69:6: "Let not those who hope in you be put to shame through me, O Lord God of hosts; let not those who seek you be brought to dishonor through me, O God of Israel."

- Micah 7:19: "He will again have compassion on us; he will tread our iniquities underfoot. You will cast all our sins into the depths of the sea."

Overcoming Shame Through Scripture

The Bible offers powerful reminders that, through faith in God, we can overcome shame and embrace the new life offered to us in Christ. Below are additional scriptures that speak to God's power to redeem and lift us out of shame:

- 2 Corinthians 5:17: "Therefore, if anyone is in Christ, he is a new creation. The old has passed away; behold, the new has come."

- Hebrews 12:2: "Looking to Jesus, the founder and perfecter of our faith, who for the joy that was set before him endured the cross, despising the shame, and is seated at the right hand of the throne of God."

- Isaiah 61:3: "To grant to those who mourn in Zion—to give them a beautiful headdress instead of ashes, the oil of gladness instead of mourning, the garment of praise instead of a faint spirit; that they may be called oaks of righteousness, the planting of the Lord, that he may be glorified."

- Joel 2:26-27: "You shall eat in plenty and be satisfied, and praise the name of the Lord your God, who has dealt wondrously with you. And my people shall never again be put to shame. You shall know that I am in the midst of Israel, and that I am the Lord your God and there is none else. And my people shall never again be put to shame."

- Zephaniah 3:17: "The Lord your God is in your midst, a mighty one who will save; he will rejoice over you with gladness; he will quiet you by his love; he will exult over you with loud singing."

- Romans 5:5: "And hope does not put us to shame, because God's love has been poured into our hearts through the Holy Spirit who has been given to us."

- Isaiah 43:25: "I, I am he who blots out your transgressions for my own sake, and I will not remember your sins."

- Jeremiah 31:34: "And no longer shall each one teach his neighbor and each his brother, saying, 'Know the Lord,' for they shall all know me, from the least of them to the greatest, declares the Lord. For I will forgive their iniquity, and I will remember their sin no more."

- 1 Peter 2:6: "For it stands in Scripture: 'Behold, I am laying in Zion a stone, a cornerstone chosen and precious, and whoever believes in him will not be put to shame.'"

- Psalm 25:3: "Indeed, none who wait for you shall be put to shame; they shall be ashamed who are wantonly treacherous."

- Isaiah 45:17: "But Israel is saved by the Lord with everlasting salvation; you shall not be put to shame or confounded to all eternity."

Embracing the New Life in Christ

As believers, we are called to leave behind the shame of our past and step into the freedom and joy that comes with a life in Christ. Here are a few key points to remember:

1. New Identity in Christ: When we accept Christ, we become new creations (2 Corinthians 5:17). Our old self, with all its shame and sin, is gone, and we are given a new identity in Him.

2. Jesus Bore Our Shame: Jesus endured the cross, despising its shame, so that we could be free from it (Hebrews 12:2). His sacrifice means that we no longer have to carry the burden of shame.

3. The Promise of Restoration: God promises to replace our shame with joy, honor, and double portions of His blessings (Isaiah 61:7). He redeems and restores us, turning our mourning into dancing.

4. Eternal Security: Those who put their trust in God will never be put to shame (Romans 10:11; 1 Peter 2:6). Our hope in Him is secure, and He is faithful to uphold us.

5. Forgiveness and Cleansing: God is faithful to forgive our sins and cleanse us from all unrighteousness (1 John 1:9). Through repentance, we are washed clean, and our sins are remembered no more (Jeremiah 31:34).

Shame, whether inherited or self-inflicted, can be a heavy burden, but God offers us freedom through Christ. By embracing the truth of Scripture and trusting in God's promises, we can overcome shame and live in the fullness of His grace and love. The journey from shame to glory is one of transformation, where the weight of the past is lifted, and we walk forward with confidence, knowing that we are loved, forgiven, and restored by our Creator.

CHAPTER 04

Individual Shame

Understanding Individual Shame

What is individual shame? Individual shame refers to the personal experience of feeling inadequate, unworthy, or ashamed of oneself. This internalized emotion can arise from various situations, such as making mistakes, experiencing failures, facing rejection, or being judged or criticized by others.

Individual shame is often marked by a sense of unworthiness, self-doubt, and the belief that one's flaws make them unlovable or undeserving of respect and acceptance. It can manifest as negative self-talk, harsh self-criticism, and a sense of disconnection from others, as well as from one's own identity and purpose.

This type of shame can be particularly challenging to overcome because it is often deeply ingrained in a person's sense of self and may be reinforced by societal or cultural expectations. However, through therapy, support groups, and other forms of treatment, individuals can learn to recognize and challenge their feelings of shame, develop a healthier sense of self-worth, and build better relationships with themselves and others.

Root of Individual Shame: Individual shame, along with imposed, institutional, and incessant shame, is rooted in the inherited sin nature and is often triggered by personal sins.

Biblical Insights on Shame

The following scriptures shed light on the sources and consequences of shame:

- Proverbs 11:2: "When pride comes, then comes disgrace, but with humility comes wisdom."

- Proverbs 13:5: "The righteous hate what is false, but the wicked make themselves a stench and bring shame on themselves."

- Proverbs 13:18: "Whoever disregards discipline comes to poverty and shame, but whoever heeds correction is honored."

These verses emphasize that those who refuse instruction and correction are likely to face shame and failure, while those who are willing to learn and grow will find success and honor.

- Proverbs 19:26: "Whoever robs their father and drives out their mother is a child who brings shame and disgrace."

- Proverbs 18:13: "To answer before listening—that is folly and shame."

- Jeremiah 17:13: "Lord, you are the hope of Israel; all who forsake you will be put to shame. Those who turn away from you will be written in the dust because they have forsaken the Lord, the spring of living water."

- Ezekiel 43:10: "Son of man, describe the temple to the people of Israel, that they may be ashamed of their sins. Let them consider its perfection."

These verses illustrate how shame can result from actions that dishonor God or others and how acknowledging one's sins can lead to a deeper understanding of God's grace.

The Alienation of Shame

Shame can alienate you from God, others, and even yourself because it is difficult to forgive yourself for sins, mistakes, and bad decisions. However, forgiving yourself is not about forgetting the past; it is about choosing not to hold your past against yourself in negative ways. Forgiveness means letting go of what you are holding against yourself so that you can move forward with God. If God has forgiven you, should you not do the same?

Philippians 4:9 urges us to put into practice the things we have learned from God's Word. Continuously rehearsing the events of our transgressions opposes Philippians 4:8, which encourages us to dwell on whatever is true, noble, right, pure, lovely, and admirable.

A Biblical Example of Individual Shame: King David's Sin with Bathsheba

King David's sin with Bathsheba is a profound example of individual shame:

1. Adultery: David brought Bathsheba, another man's wife, to the palace and had intimate relations with her.

2. Deception: David tried to cover up his sin by summoning Uriah, Bathsheba's husband, encouraging him to spend the night with her. When Uriah refused, David's plan failed.

3. Murder: David arranged for Uriah to be placed at the front lines of battle, ensuring his death.

The story of David and Bathsheba teaches us several important lessons:

1. Hidden sins will eventually be exposed.

2. God forgives those who repent.

3. The consequences of sin remain even after forgiveness.

4. God can bring about good even in difficult situations. For example, David and Bathsheba's next son, Solomon, became the heir to the throne.

5. God's plans always serve His sovereign purpose, even in the midst of human failures.

Shame can also have physical effects. As seen in David's case, his shame led to depression, guilt, and physical suffering: "When I kept silent, my bones wasted away through my groaning all day long. For day and night your hand was heavy on me; my strength was sapped as in the heat of summer" (Psalm 32:3-4).

Shame is often referred to as a "silent killer." It can cause physiological responses, including increased cortisol levels, which can lead to elevated heart rates and constricted arteries. People who struggle to forgive themselves may never move beyond their past, and the burden of shame can eventually take a toll on their health.

Nathan's Parable and David's Sin

To confront David's unconfessed sin, the prophet Nathan used a parable about a rich man who, instead of slaughtering one of his own many flocks, took a poor man's only lamb to prepare a meal for a traveler. This story exposed David's sin, leading him to repentance.

David's story serves as a reminder of the importance of acknowledging and repenting of our sins, as well as the physical and emotional toll that unconfessed shame can take on our lives.

The Process of Repentance and Restoration

David's response to Nathan's parable was one of genuine repentance. Psalm 51 is a powerful expression of David's remorse and his plea for God's mercy:

- Psalm 51:1-2: "Have mercy on me, O God, according to your unfailing love; according to your great compassion blot out my transgressions. Wash away all my iniquity and cleanse me from my sin."

In this psalm, David acknowledges his sin, expresses deep sorrow, and seeks cleansing and renewal from God. His words reflect a heart that is broken over sin but also one that trusts in God's ability to forgive and restore.

David's journey from shame to restoration illustrates the process of repentance and the hope of redemption:

1. Acknowledgment of Sin: David did not deny or minimize his sin. He confessed it openly to God, recognizing the gravity of his actions.

2. Seeking Forgiveness: David's plea for mercy shows his understanding that only God can cleanse him from his sin and remove his guilt.

3. Desire for Renewal: David asked God to create a pure heart within him and renew a steadfast spirit (Psalm 51:10). This reflects a longing not just for forgiveness, but for a transformation that would align his heart with God's will.

4. Commitment to Change: David's repentance was not just a one-time event. It involved a commitment to turn away from sin and to live a life that honored God.

The Physical and Emotional Impact of Shame

David's experience highlights the profound physical and emotional impact that shame can have on an individual. In Psalm 32, David describes how keeping silent about his sin led to physical deterioration and emotional anguish:

- Psalm 32:3-4: "When I kept silent, my bones wasted away through my groaning all day long. For day and night your hand was heavy on me; my strength was sapped as in the heat of summer."

The weight of unconfessed sin can lead to a range of physical symptoms, including fatigue, stress, and even illness. This passage underscores the importance of confession and the release it brings—not just spiritually, but physically and emotionally as well.

Forgiving Yourself and Moving Forward

One of the most challenging aspects of dealing with shame is forgiving yourself. As David's story shows, God is willing to forgive our sins when we truly repent. However, moving past shame also requires that we forgive ourselves.

Forgiving yourself is not about forgetting the past but about refusing to allow past mistakes to define you. It means letting go of self-condemnation and embracing the forgiveness that God offers. This can be a difficult process, but it is essential for healing and moving forward.

- Philippians 3:13-14: "Brothers and sisters, I do not consider myself yet to have taken hold of it. But one thing I do: Forgetting what is behind and straining toward what is ahead, I press on toward the goal to win the prize for which God has called me heavenward in Christ Jesus."

Paul's words encourage us to leave behind the mistakes of the past and to focus on the future that God has in store for us. By doing so, we can break free from the cycle of shame and live in the freedom that Christ offers.

The Role of Faith-Based Counseling

For those struggling with deep-seated shame, faith-based counseling can be an invaluable resource. Such counseling seeks to uncover the lies that individuals believe about themselves—lies that keep them trapped in shame— and replace those lies with the truth of God's Word.

Counselors help individuals recognize that their worth is not determined by their past mistakes but by their identity in Christ. By guiding them through Scripture, prayer, and the healing power of God's love, counselors can help those burdened by shame find freedom and restoration.

Shame, whether it arises from personal sin, societal expectations, or the judgment of others, can be a crippling force. However, the Bible provides a clear path to overcoming shame through confession, repentance, and the acceptance of God's forgiveness.

David's journey from shame to redemption serves as a powerful reminder that no matter how great our sin, God's grace is greater. When we turn to Him in repentance, He is faithful to forgive, cleanse, and restore us.

By embracing the forgiveness that God offers and by learning to forgive ourselves, we can move forward into the future that God has prepared for us—a future free from the burden of shame and filled with the hope of His love and redemption.

CHAPTER 05

Incessant Shame

Understanding Incessant Shame

What is incessant shame? Incessant shame is a relentless and overwhelming feeling of inadequacy and self-blame that seems impossible to escape. This deep-seated emotion often manifests as persistent self-criticism and a pervasive sense of worthlessness.

Incessant shame can stem from a variety of sources, including childhood trauma, chronic stress, mental health conditions like depression or anxiety, or ongoing pressure from societal or cultural expectations. Those experiencing incessant shame often feel as though they are never good enough, constantly falling short of expectations, and inherently flawed or unworthy of love and acceptance. This can lead to a cycle of negative self-talk, self-isolation, and avoidance of positive experiences or relationships.

Overcoming incessant shame typically requires a multifaceted approach, including therapy, medication, and lifestyle changes. Cognitive-behavioral therapy (CBT) and other forms of talk therapy can be effective in helping individuals identify and challenge negative thought patterns, while medications like antidepressants or anti-anxiety drugs may help manage symptoms. Additionally, engaging in self-care, positive social activities, and hobbies can help individuals build a healthier sense of self-worth and break the cycle of incessant shame.

How is incessant shame perpetuated through generations? This continuous cycle of shame can be passed from one generation to the next, especially when shame-based parents unintentionally transfer their unresolved shame onto their children. As the saying goes, "You cannot teach self-value if you do not value yourself."

A Real-Life Example of Incessant Shame

Consider the story of a man who was severely injured in a car accident, resulting in a traumatic brain injury. Although he survived, his cognitive abilities were reduced to the level of a child, leaving him unable to read, drive, or live independently. He now lives with his parents and, feeling lonely, seeks out neighbors to talk to. However, because his conversation is childlike, many avoid him.

His mother is nurturing and supportive, but his father struggles to accept his son's disability. The father blames his son for not being able to do more, and this criticism only serves to discourage and frustrate the son, reinforcing his feelings of shame.

It seems likely that the father is projecting his own guilt and shame onto his son. He was the one driving the night of the accident, and his inability to process his own feelings of guilt and shame has led him to criticize his son instead. This is a classic example of how unresolved shame can be transferred from one person to another, creating a destructive cycle.

Breaking the Cycle of Shame

To prevent the transmission of shame to future generations, it is crucial to address and resolve it. In the example above, the father's shame likely triggered feelings of low self-esteem and unworthiness, leading to self-sabotaging behaviors like starting arguments, intense anger, or other forms of abuse. His negative behavior towards his son likely reinforces his own shame, creating a vicious cycle.

Steps toward healing:

1. Confession and Forgiveness: The father's healing should begin with confessing his sins to God. While the accident itself may not have been a sin (unless it involved reckless behavior, such as driving under the influence), his subsequent treatment of his son certainly is. According to Jeremiah 31:34, when God forgives us, He chooses not to remember our sins in a negative way. This means that God, in His infinite wisdom, does not continually bring up our past mistakes.

2. Self-Forgiveness: The father must also forgive himself. This involves reframing his thoughts about the accident, acknowledging it as a tragic event that cannot be changed. If he is still second-guessing his actions in the moments leading up to the accident, he must recognize that those thoughts serve no purpose now. It's time to let go and move forward.

3. Apology: While the father might consider apologizing to his son, he should assess whether his son is emotionally mature enough to process such a conversation. Even if the son cannot fully comprehend it, an apology might still serve as a bonding moment between them.

4. Patience and Compassion: As the father begins to forgive himself, he may find it easier to interact with his son with greater patience, compassion, and acceptance.

The Impact of Shame on Intimacy: Shame can severely hinder intimacy and make it difficult to maintain close relationships. When you feel defective or flawed, it becomes challenging to open up to others. Intimacy between partners grows as they build trust and express their true selves to each other. However, when shame enters the picture, it can lead to secrecy and hiding—especially of actions or feelings you believe your partner might judge. Ironically, discussing feelings of shame with your spouse can be a deeply intimate and healing gesture, fostering greater closeness and understanding.

By confronting and addressing shame, individuals can break free from its grip and build healthier, more fulfilling relationships with themselves and others.

What is meant by the term "heredity"?

"Heredity" is the term given to the means by which living organisms reproduce after their own kind.

The term "heredity" refers to the passing of genetic traits or characteristics from one generation to the next. It is the transmission of genetic information from parents to offspring through the process of reproduction.

Heredity plays a fundamental role in determining the physical and biological characteristics of an individual, including eye color, hair color, height, susceptibility to certain diseases, and more. The traits that are passed down from parents to offspring are determined by the genetic material carried by the parents' DNA.

The study of heredity is known as genetics, and it is an important area of study in biology and other fields. Understanding heredity can help us understand how traits are inherited and can lead to advancements in fields such as medicine and agriculture, including the development of treatments for genetic diseases and the creation of genetically modified crops.

Are physical problems transmitted from generation to generation?

It is evident that physical problems are transmitted from generation to generation through heredity.

Are spiritual problems transmitted from generation to generation?

Yes, is transmittable, this is why spiritual tendencies have multi-generational consequences.

Accordingly, "generational heredity" is the integral of Chemical and environmental heredity affecting your physical body and spiritual heredity affecting your soul and spirit. The Bible describes the spiritual forces behind inherited criminal behavior, hereditary illness, and recurring social problems as "curses" or "strongholds" of Satan.

Furthermore, generational heredity can affect you spiritually: The Infallible Word teaches that man's spiritual heredity is influenced by invisible forces. Exhibit: "...I am a jealous God, visiting the iniquity of the fathers on the children to the third and fourth generations of those who hate me." (Exodus 20:5)

What is the law of "culpability"?

Is "responsibility for wrong or error" The law of culpability, also known as the principle of culpability or the principle of fault, is a fundamental legal principle that holds individuals accountable for their actions or inactions that cause harm or damage.

Under this principle, a person can only be held responsible for their actions if they had the necessary level of intent or knowledge to understand the consequences of their actions. For example, if a person commits a crime but did not have the intent to harm anyone, they may not be held liable for the same level of punishment as someone who acted with full intent to cause harm.

The principle of culpability is important in determining the level of punishment or liability for a crime or civil offense. It is often used in criminal law to determine the degree of criminal liability, and in civil law to determine whether a defendant can be held liable for damages or compensation.

The principle of culpability is also closely tied to the concept of "men's rea", which refers to the mental state of a defendant at the time of a crime or offense. Together, these legal concepts help ensure that individuals are held accountable for their actions only to the extent that they are responsible for the harm caused.

The Bible states that while every man will answer for his own sin, weaknesses can also be transmitted to succeeding generations and become spiritual strongholds.

In Proverbs 26:2 we learn about curses as it declares, "...The curse causeless shall not come."
How is a "stronghold" created?

This is when Satan establishes residency and expands his base of operations to succeeding generations. The bondage grows stronger in each generation; hence a "stronghold" of the enemy is entrenched.

A stronghold is a fortress of thoughts that controls and influences our attitudes. They color how we view certain situations, circumstances, or people. When these thoughts and activities become habitual, we allow a spiritual fortress to be built around us. We become so used to responding to the "voice" of that spirit, that its place in our minds is secure. All of this happens on a subconscious level, and it is one of Satan's favorite weapons. Since we tend to pass our own pattern of thinking and views on to our children, the cycle continues.

Why does shame grow worse with each succeeding generation?

Shame can grow worse with each succeeding generation due to a variety of factors, including intergenerational trauma and cultural or societal pressures.

Intergenerational trauma refers to the transmission of trauma or other negative experiences from one generation to the next, often through the sharing of stories, cultural practices, or familial behaviors. For example, if a family has a history of abuse or addiction, the children of that family may experience shame and other negative emotions related to those experiences, even if they did not directly experience the trauma themselves.

Cultural or societal pressures can also contribute to the worsening of shame across generations. For example, if a society places a high value on certain traits or accomplishments, such as academic or career success, individuals who do not meet those standards may feel shame or inadequacy. Over time, these societal pressures can become entrenched, leading to increasingly high standards and expectations that can be difficult to meet.

In addition, shame can be passed down from one generation to the next through family dynamics and interpersonal relationships. For example, a parent who experiences shame may inadvertently pass those feelings down to their children through criticism or unrealistic expectations. Over time, these patterns can become entrenched and perpetuate across generations.

Breaking the cycle of intergenerational shame requires a combination of individual and societal change. This may include therapy and other forms of mental health support, addressing societal pressures and cultural norms that contribute to shame, and building healthier family and interpersonal relationships.

Accordingly, shame will grow worse when is left unchallenged, shame will be passed on incessantly using your "house"--your generational heritage--as the mode of transmission--and it will grow increasingly stronger in each generation.

Consequently, curse was passed on in David's family through the cycle of shame of similar sins being committed by David's sons. The "curse" was passed on and the cycle of shame continued. As Exhibited in 2 Samuel 13:1-2 We find David's son, Amnon, tempted with the same sin his father battled, lusting for a woman he could not have.

The truly amazing testimony of David's life is that, after this sequence of sins, he repented. And because of his deep repentance without making excuses, God extended grace and forgiveness. However, unfortunately, David and his family still experienced the tragic consequences of his sin.

- David's child, born to Bathsheba, died.
- David's daughter, Tamar, was raped by her half-brother, Amnon.
- Absalom, David's son/Tamar's brother, murdered Amnon.
- Absalom rebelled against David and slept with his concubines.
- Absalom attempted to dethrone David and was murdered in the process.
- The division of the once unified kingdom began.

David's shame must have been compounded by the awareness that his sin ultimately killed his sons. Even so, although the consequences of his sin were continually before him, David himself lived with confidence before God for the remainder of his days - because he personally understood forgiveness.

CHAPTER 06

Imposed Shame

Understanding Imposed Shame

What is imposed shame? Imposed shame occurs when shame is inflicted upon an individual by external forces, such as societal or cultural expectations, family dynamics, or interpersonal relationships. Unlike internalized shame, which arises from an individual's own self-perception, imposed shame is often beyond the individual's control.

Imposed shame can manifest in various ways. For example, a person may feel ashamed due to characteristics such as race, gender, or sexual orientation—traits that society might stigmatize. Additionally, family dynamics can contribute to imposed shame, such as when someone is made to feel inadequate for not meeting their parents' expectations or for being unfavorably compared to siblings.

This type of shame can be particularly harmful because it is continually reinforced by external sources, making it challenging for individuals to escape or confront. As a result, it can lead to feelings of powerlessness, low self-esteem, and self-doubt, potentially contributing to a range of mental health issues.

Addressing imposed shame often requires both individual and societal efforts. This might involve seeking therapy and mental health support, challenging cultural norms and societal expectations that perpetuate shame, and fostering healthier family and interpersonal relationships.

In essence, imposed shame is inflicted by others who belittle, criticize, or tell you that you are not good enough. It communicates the message, "You have disappointed us. You are a bad person." This is rooted in the belief that one's identity and actions are inherently flawed.

The Nature of Imposed Shame

Imposed shame can manifest in various ways, often delivered with subtle or implicit cruelty. For instance, laughing at someone's mistake or humiliating them in front of a group serves no constructive purpose. The question is, who benefits from such actions? Certainly not the person who was shamed. Typically, imposed shame benefits the person inflicting it, as a means of asserting power and control in social interactions or relationships.

The Roots of Imposed Shame:

The seeds of imposed shame are often planted during childhood through experiences that reinforce feelings of worthlessness. These experiences can include:

1. Religion: Strict religious regulations that dictate adherence to certain traditions to be deemed acceptable.

2. Identification with Shame-Based Models: As humans, we have an innate need to belong to something greater than ourselves. According to John Bradshaw, "With

the exception of self-preservation, no other striving is as compelling as this need, which begins with our caregivers and extends to family, peer groups, culture, nation, and the world." Shame is deeply relational, often instilled by those with whom we have significant relationships—parents, teachers, peers, bosses—who make us feel inadequate.

3. Accusations, Abandonment, and Abuse: Accusations can be subtle, delivered through facial expressions, tones of voice, and pious rebukes, yet they communicate rejection as clearly as if it were publicly announced. Abandonment, whether by parents or a spouse, also leads to imposed shame, as the abandoned individual often blames themselves for the relationship's end. Physical, verbal, and emotional abuse reinforce a child's belief that they are bad, stupid, and worthless, creating a strong foundation for shame.

The Impact of Childhood Shaming

Shaming and humiliating children is a form of emotional abuse that can have long-lasting effects. Children subjected to this kind of treatment grow up feeling unloved, unwanted, and fearful. Their normal development is interrupted, and negative internal messages, such as "I'm not good enough," become ingrained.

When these children grow up and become parents, they often raise their own children in the same manner. The messages they internalized in childhood play like a broken record, repeating in the ears of their children: "How could you be so stupid?" "You can't do anything right." "This is why no one likes you."

Historical Example of Imposed Shame: The Dunce Cap

In the Victorian era, a child who failed to do their homework or misbehaved in class was often sent to sit on a stool in the corner of the classroom, forced to wear a cone-shaped hat labeled "dunce" or marked with a large letter "D." This served not only as a punishment for the child but also as a warning to other students. It is a classic example of imposed shame by a teacher.

A New Testament Example of Imposed Shame: The Woman Caught in Adultery

A powerful illustration of imposed shame in the New Testament is the story of the woman caught in adultery, as described in John 8:3-6. The scribes and Pharisees brought her before Jesus, stating, "Teacher, this woman was caught in adultery, in the very act. Now Moses, in the law, commanded us that such should be stoned. But what do You say?" This scenario was a trap, designed to test Jesus. The religious leaders knew that both the adulterous man and woman were required by the Law of Moses to be stoned, yet they only presented the woman, likely because the man was a religious leader who had set her up to challenge Jesus.

The religious leaders' response was the typical voice of legalistic religion, proclaiming, "You deserve to die." However, Jesus' response was entirely different. He did not condemn her but instead said, "Woman, where are those accusers of yours? Has no one condemned you?" She replied, "No one, Lord." And Jesus said, "Neither do I condemn you; go and sin no more."

When the religious leaders left, they effectively "dropped the charges" against the woman. Only Jesus remained, the only sinless one qualified to judge her. Yet, instead of condemning her, He extended mercy and commanded her to change her ways. Jesus recognized her sin, but He also understood that forgiveness would lead to transformation.

This story highlights the contrast between imposed shame and the grace offered by Jesus. While the religious leaders sought to impose shame and condemnation, Jesus offered forgiveness and the opportunity for a new beginning.

The Power of Forgiveness in Overcoming Imposed Shame

The story of the woman caught in adultery not only illustrates the harmful effects of imposed shame but also highlights the transformative power of forgiveness. While the religious leaders were quick to impose shame and judgment, Jesus offered a path to redemption. His approach underscores an important truth: shame, whether imposed by others or internalized, does not have to define us. Through forgiveness—both divine and self-initiated—we can break free from the cycle of shame and embrace a new life.

Jesus' Example of Grace and Compassion:

Jesus' refusal to condemn the woman caught in adultery is a powerful example of grace and compassion. He acknowledged her sin but chose to forgive rather than judge. This act of mercy was not just about pardoning her past but about empowering her future. Jesus knew that true change comes not from condemnation but from the experience of unconditional love and forgiveness. His command to "go and sin no more" was a call to leave behind a life of shame and to step into a new identity shaped by grace.

The Lasting Effects of Imposed Shame

Imposed shame, especially when reinforced by authority figures or cultural norms, can have lasting effects on an individual's psyche. It can create a deep-seated belief that one is inherently flawed, unworthy, or deserving of mistreatment. Over time, this can lead to a range of emotional and psychological issues, including:

1. Low Self-Esteem: People who have experienced imposed shame often struggle with feelings of inadequacy and unworthiness. They may internalize the negative messages they receive, believing that they are not deserving of love, respect, or success.

2. Anxiety and Depression: The constant fear of judgment and the belief that one is inherently flawed can lead to chronic anxiety and depression. These conditions are often exacerbated by the isolation that accompanies imposed shame, as individuals withdraw from relationships and opportunities to avoid further humiliation.

3. Relationship Difficulties: Imposed shame can make it difficult to form healthy relationships. Individuals may struggle with trust, fear vulnerability, or feel unworthy of love and support. This can lead to a cycle of unhealthy relationships, where the person either avoids closeness altogether or becomes involved in relationships that reinforce their sense of shame.

4. Perfectionism: In an attempt to avoid shame, some individuals may develop perfectionistic tendencies. They believe that by being perfect, they can shield themselves from criticism and rejection. However, this often leads to a constant state of stress and anxiety, as perfection is an unattainable goal.

Breaking the Cycle of Imposed Shame

Breaking free from imposed shame requires a multifaceted approach that includes both individual healing and broader societal change. Here are some steps that can help in overcoming imposed shame:

1. Seek Therapy: Professional counseling can help individuals identify and challenge the negative beliefs that have been instilled in them. Cognitive-behavioral therapy (CBT), in particular, is effective in helping people reframe their thoughts and develop healthier self-perceptions.

2. Build Supportive Relationships: Surrounding oneself with supportive, nonjudgmental people can help counteract the effects of imposed shame. These relationships provide a safe space for individuals to express their true selves without fear of ridicule or rejection.

3. Challenge Societal Norms: On a broader level, it is important to challenge the societal and cultural norms that perpetuate shame. This might involve advocating for more inclusive and accepting communities, where diversity is celebrated rather than stigmatized.

4. Practice Self-Compassion: Learning to treat oneself with kindness and understanding is crucial in overcoming shame. Self-compassion involves recognizing that everyone makes mistakes and that these mistakes do not define one's worth. It's about giving oneself the grace to be imperfect.

5. Embrace Forgiveness: Forgiving oneself and others is a key step in breaking free from shame. This doesn't mean condoning harmful behavior, but rather letting go of the negative emotions that keep one trapped in a cycle of shame and resentment.

A Path to Healing: Moving Beyond Imposed Shame

The journey to healing from imposed shame is not easy, but it is possible. By following the example of Jesus—who offers forgiveness instead of condemnation—we can begin to dismantle the lies that shame has built in our lives. Forgiveness, both received from God and extended to ourselves and others, is a powerful tool in this process.

As we embrace the truth that we are loved and valued by God, regardless of our past mistakes or the judgments of others, we can begin to live in the freedom that comes from knowing our true worth. This freedom allows us to build healthier relationships, pursue our goals without fear of failure, and experience the joy and peace that come from living a life unburdened by shame.

In conclusion, while imposed shame can have devastating effects, it is not insurmountable. Through a combination of therapy, supportive relationships, self-compassion, and a deep understanding of God's grace, individuals can overcome the effects of imposed shame and move forward into a life of greater freedom, peace, and fulfillment.

CHAPTER 07

Institutional Shame

Understanding Institutional Shame

What is institutional shame? Institutional shame refers to a type of shame that is rooted in the standards and judgments of organizations, systems, or institutions, rather than in individual actions. This form of shame is based on societal concepts of right and wrong, acceptable and unacceptable behaviors, as dictated by the collective values and norms of a particular group or society.

For example, consider the issue of abortion. Although abortion has been legal in the United States for over 40 years, the stigma and shame associated with it remain significant. A woman who has had an abortion might feel ashamed to disclose her experience to a fellow church member, burdened by guilt for ending a life, and haunted by the sadness of never knowing the child she could have raised. She may also feel isolated, believing there is no one she can confide in about her experience.

Institutional Shame Explained:

Institutional shame arises from the actions or policies of an organization, system, or institution that are perceived as harmful or inconsistent with widely held ethical standards. This type of shame is not tied to an individual's personal actions but to the collective behavior or decisions of the institution to which they belong.

Institutional shame can occur in various contexts, such as:

- Government Agencies: When a government body is discovered to have engaged in systemic discrimination or corruption.

- Religious Organizations: When a religious institution is involved in a scandal, such as covering up abuse.

- Corporate Settings: When a company is found guilty of unethical business practices or causing environmental damage.

Consequences of Institutional Shame:

Institutional shame can have far-reaching consequences, affecting both the organization and the individuals associated with it. These consequences may include:

- Loss of Trust and Credibility: Stakeholders may lose faith in the institution, leading to diminished trust and credibility.

- Reputation Damage: The organization's reputation and brand image can suffer significant harm, leading to long-term impacts.

- Legal and Financial Penalties: Institutions may face legal action, fines, or other financial repercussions as a result of their actions.

Addressing Institutional Shame:

To effectively address institutional shame, both individual and systemic changes are often necessary. Steps may include:

- Commitment to Transparency and Accountability: Organizations must be open about their actions and hold themselves accountable for past mistakes.

- Policy and Practice Reforms: Revising policies and practices that have contributed to harm or unethical behavior is essential for regaining trust.

- Restitution: Providing compensation or support to those affected by the institution's actions is a critical part of the healing process.

- Cultural Shifts: Promoting greater awareness of the social and ethical responsibilities of organizations and emphasizing the importance of social justice and accountability can help prevent future instances of institutional shame.

In summary, institutional shame is a reflection of the collective actions or policies of an organization that conflict with societal values and ethics. Addressing this shame requires comprehensive efforts to reform practices, rebuild trust, and promote a culture of responsibility and transparency.

How does it result in our lives?

It results when we are rejected by the group or when our group is rejected by another or our culture at large.

For example, special interest groups are good at (and take pride in) shining the light on corporations causing harm to the environment by dumping toxins. The government may impose large fines, but media shaming and boycotting such businesses may have a greater impact on the decision-makers.

One of the examples of a shame-based society is that shame belittles you because of your personal background, your family, where you live, or the way you dress.

Another example that came to my mind is the practice of shunning by the Amish. Amish shunning is the use of social exclusion as the method used to enforce Amish church rules. When you are shunned:

- Amish members may no longer eat at the same table with you. This means that, if you attend an Amish gathering like a wedding or funeral, you must sit apart from the Church members when food is served.
- Members may not do business with you. This can be a real hardship if you buy from and sell to your Amish neighbors.
- Members may not ride in your car. If you visit your family, they are forbidden to ride with you, even though they are allowed to ride with their "English" neighbor.
- Members cannot receive anything from you. Friends and family can help you by giving you money or things that you need. But they are forbidden to accept anything from you. So, for example, if you want to serve a glass of water to your parents, you must leave it on the table for one of your younger siblings to give to your parents. Since your siblings are not yet members of the Amish church, they are not yet bound to the rules applying to shunning.

Amish Shunning is based on Paul's teaching in 1 Corinthians 5:9-12.

How does institutional shame relate to scapegoating?

Is a shame-based response by discharging the guilt and shame right back to God.

Institutional shame can be related to scapegoating in several ways. Scapegoating is the act of blaming an individual or group for a problem or issue, often in a way that is unfair or unjustified. This can be done in order to deflect blame or responsibility away from an institution or organization.

For example, if a company is found to have engaged in unethical business practices, it may attempt to scapegoat individual employees or a particular department, rather than acknowledging that the problem was systemic and rooted in the company's culture or policies. This allows the organization to avoid taking responsibility for the harm it has caused and may perpetuate a culture of blame and avoidance.

In some cases, institutional shame can also be the result of scapegoating. For example, if a group or organization is unfairly blamed for a problem or issue, this can lead to feelings of shame and guilt, even if the accusations are unfounded or exaggerated.

Addressing institutional shame and scapegoating requires a commitment to transparency, accountability, and fairness. This may include a willingness to acknowledge and take responsibility for mistakes or harm caused, as well as a commitment to addressing underlying issues and promoting a culture of respect and ethical behavior. It may also require efforts to challenge and correct false or misleading narratives that contribute to scapegoating and institutional shame.

What is the ultimate manifestation of unresolved institutional shame?

It produces shameless conduct leading to a mob mentality and brutality such as that demonstrated by Hitler's forces in World War II.

Why institutional shame must be dealt with in order to wage effective spiritual warfare.: Guilt that has never been dealt with is an open invitation to demonic powers. Before we can bind the strongman, we need to deal with the sins that have given the enemy a legal right to occupy. The devil and his principalities have been defeated by Jesus on the cross and they would not be able to stay on unless they were relying on old invitations that have never been canceled.

Explain the importance of repenting for corporate sins as well as your own individual sins.: Wagner explains: When that happens, God can pour out His Holy Spirit. It then becomes easier for unbelievers to hear the gospel of Christ, repent of their personal sins, and be saved. This is how strategic-level intercession paves the way for effective evangelism.

Explain how Jesus experienced institutional shame.: Jesus also endured the shame surrounding the circumstances of his birth, having been conceived by Mary through the Holy Spirit prior to her marriage to Joseph. In one confrontation the Pharisees boasted, "We were not born of fornication" (John 8:41).

At one time, a friend of mine worked at a hotel in the Caribbean with 500 employees. About 90% of the hotel employees were West Indian, with varying skin shades from tan to black. In the past, the name of the Caribbean Island from which they came was included on their name tags. However, in about 2001, the management decided to make everyone a new name tag - without the name of the island, state, or country from which they came.

The islanders had their own hierarchy of degrees of status attached to islands – and a person enjoyed a higher ranking of social status if they were from one island rather than another. There started to be frequent fights among the employees when one would bully or mock the other because of the island they were from. Yes – I'm talking about adults!

Here is another example, and I personally saw this in one of the hotels. Research has found extensive evidence of discrimination among blacks based on skin tone in criminal justice, business, labor market, housing, health care, media and politics in the United States and Europe. Lighter skin tones are seen as preferable and given a greater degree of deference and respect, in many instances resulting in better jobs.

One of the Old Testament examples to illustrate institutional shame is the story of Rahab: Rahab was—a prostitute living an openly sinful life. Every night that she brought another stranger into her bed, guilt must have weighed her down even more heavily than the men. Every morning as she woke up to a cold empty bed and placed the money from the night's deeds in their place of safekeeping, she must have felt repulsed by what she had done. Selling her body to men who would never bring her the kind of safety and security she was looking for was only one sign of the sin that stained her heart and soul. Although Rahab escaped the destruction of Jericho, she still carried the institutional shame of being a harlot.

When the walls of Jericho fell down and the Israelites took the city, Joshua commanded that Rahab and her family be spared (Joshua 6:22–23). Marking her home was, of course, the "cord of scarlet thread." It's easy to dismiss the color of Rahab's rope as a mere coincidence, but the scarlet color is significant. The rope in her window was a sign of her faith and led to her salvation, as she was not destroyed with the rest of Jericho.

What was the symbolic meaning of the scarlet cord?

In the Bible, the scarlet cord is a symbol of redemption and salvation. In the book of Joshua, the Israelite spies are aided by Rahab, a prostitute living in the city of Jericho. In return for her help, the spies promise to spare Rahab and her family when the Israelites conquer the city. They instruct her to tie a scarlet cord in her window so that they can identify her house and spare those inside.

The scarlet cord represents the redemption and salvation offered by God to all who believe in him. It is a symbol of the blood of Jesus Christ, which was shed for the forgiveness of sins and the salvation of all who trust in him. The scarlet color also represents the atonement and purification from sin, as well as the royalty and victory of Christ.

The scarlet cord can also be seen as a symbol of faith and obedience. Rahab demonstrated her faith by believing in the God of the Israelites and acting on that faith by helping the spies. She also demonstrated obedience by following the instructions given to her by the spies, which resulted in her salvation and the salvation of her family.

Overall, the scarlet cord represents the grace, mercy, and salvation offered by God to all who put their faith in him and follow his commands.

The scarlet cord from Rahab's window was certainly a symbol of redemption through the blood and the promise of God, "When I see the blood, I will pass over you" (Exodus 12:13).

The scarlet rope—the color of blood—worked for Rahab much as the blood of the Passover lamb had worked during the exodus. Every home marked with blood was spared death that night (Exodus 12:13). God's mercy and forgiveness of Rahab the harlot was signified by a rope of scarlet thread, which became a symbol of the blood of Christ.

CHAPTER 08

Shattering The Obstacles

Four Steps to Overcoming Shame

1. Acknowledge Your Shame:

The first step in dealing with shame is to acknowledge it. Denying or ignoring shame will not make it go away. You must courageously admit your shame, facing it head-on.

2. Act Against Your Shame:

Once you've acknowledged your shame, take action against it by repenting of the things that caused it. True repentance involves an internal decision that leads to an outward change, turning away from sin. As David said, "I will declare my iniquity; I will be in anguish over my sin" (Psalms 38:18). He asked God to search his heart and cleanse him from secret sins (Psalms 139:23-24).

3. Address Your Shame:

After acknowledging and acting against your shame, it's important to address it directly. Like David, speak words of truth to counter the lingering accusations of shame. He said, "I acknowledged my sin to You, and my iniquity I have not hidden. I said, 'I will confess my transgressions to the Lord.' And You forgave the iniquity of my sin" (Psalms 32:5).

4. Seek an Intimate Relationship with God:

Finally, seek a deep, personal relationship with God. The only way to fully break free from the power of shame is through a close, intimate connection with Him. Faith in the work and promises of Christ is the key to overcoming shame. While shame declares us guilty and deficient, Jesus declares us guiltless and promises that His grace is sufficient for all our weaknesses (2 Corinthians 12:9-10). As we trust in Jesus as our righteousness (Philippians 3:9) and provider (Philippians 4:19), shame loses its grip on us.

Biblical Examples of Overcoming Shame

1. Inherited Shame – Paul:

The Apostle Paul confronted his inherited shame, moved beyond condemnation, and became one of the greatest advocates of God's grace in the New Testament.

2. Individual Shame – David:

David acknowledged his personal sin and repented. An example of individual shame is also seen in the woman who suffered from a hemorrhage for twelve years. Unclean and isolated, she sought healing from Jesus, but in secret. Jesus, however, made her openly acknowledge her situation, turning her shame into a testimony of His grace (Luke 8:43-48).

3. Incessant Shame – David:

The ongoing shame that plagued David's lineage was ultimately reversed, leading to the birth of Jesus Christ. David, despite his sin of adultery and murder, confessed and repented, and his guilt and shame were paid for in full through the pre-incarnate Christ (2 Samuel 11, 12:13).

4. Imposed Shame – The Adulterous Woman:

The woman caught in adultery dealt with imposed shame by seeking forgiveness and transforming her life. Although her life had been filled with shame, Jesus did not deny her sin but forgave it and offered her a fresh start (John 8:3-11).

5. Institutional Shame – Rahab:

Rahab, who was stigmatized by her profession, acted against the institutional shame of her past by recognizing and aligning herself with the God of Israel. By faith, she hid the Israelite spies, and her actions led to her and her family's salvation. Rahab's transformation from a life of shame to one of honor symbolizes the change that comes when we commit our lives to God (Joshua 2, Hebrews 11:31).

Declarations of Freedom from Shame

- Paul: Declared victory over his inherited shame with the proclamation, "There is no condemnation" (Romans 8:1).

- David: Confessed his sin and affirmed, "You forgave the iniquity of my sin" (Psalms 32:5).

- The Woman Caught in Adultery: After her imposed shame was lifted, she could declare, "No one has condemned me" (John 8:11).

- Rahab: Broke the power of institutional shame through her confession of faith, symbolized by the scarlet cord she hung in her window (Joshua 2:18-21).

These examples show that anyone can experience the wonderful release from shame. All it requires is a child-like, wholehearted belief in Jesus (John 14:1).

The Transformative Power of Faith in Overcoming Shame

Shame, whether inherited, individual, incessant, imposed, or institutional, can be a powerful and crippling force in our lives. Yet, the Bible offers numerous examples of how faith in God and His promises can transform lives burdened by shame into lives filled with grace, freedom, and purpose.

Key Principles for Breaking Free from Shame

1. Faith in Christ's Work:

The foundation for overcoming any form of shame lies in the work of Christ. Jesus' sacrifice on the cross has the power to cleanse us from all unrighteousness and free us from the chains of shame. When we place our faith in Him, we are declared righteous before God, no longer condemned by our past sins or the judgments of others. As Paul says in Romans 8:1, "There is therefore now no condemnation for those who are in Christ Jesus."

2. The Power of Confession and Repentance:

Confession and repentance are crucial steps in addressing shame. Acknowledging our sins before God and turning away from them allows us to experience His forgiveness and healing. David's life is a testament to this truth. Despite his grave sins, he found forgiveness and restoration by openly confessing his transgressions and seeking God's mercy (Psalms 51:1-2).

3. Speaking Truth to Counter Shame:

After acknowledging and repenting of our sins, it's essential to speak God's truth over our lives to counter the accusations of shame. David, after confessing his sin, declared God's forgiveness, saying, "You forgave the iniquity of my sin" (Psalms 32:5). Similarly, we must remind ourselves of God's promises and affirm our new identity in Christ, rejecting the lies of shame that tell us we are unworthy or unforgivable.

4. Building an Intimate Relationship with God:

An intimate relationship with God is the key to breaking free from shame's dominion. The closer we draw to Him, the more we understand our true worth and identity in Christ. This intimacy with God empowers us to reject shame and embrace the freedom and joy that comes from being His beloved children. As we grow in our faith, we learn to trust in Jesus as our righteousness and provider, and shame loses its power over us.

The Journey from Shame to Freedom: Biblical Examples

- Paul: Overcame inherited shame through his faith in Christ, becoming a powerful advocate for God's grace and a living example of redemption. His declaration, "There is no condemnation," serves as a reminder that our past does not define us when we are in Christ.

- David: Conquered individual shame by confessing his sins and receiving God's forgiveness. His story reminds us that no matter how great our sins, God's grace is greater, and His forgiveness is complete.

- The Hemorrhaging Woman: Despite her incessant shame, she reached out to Jesus in faith, and her shame was transformed into a testimony of healing and grace. Jesus made her public confession a moment of profound restoration.

- The Adulterous Woman: Faced with imposed shame, she found forgiveness and a new beginning in Jesus. His words, "Neither do I condemn you," set her free from the shame that had defined her life.

- Rahab: Overcame institutional shame by placing her faith in the God of Israel. Her courageous actions and declaration of faith not only saved her family but also secured her place in the lineage of Christ, demonstrating that faith can redeem any past.

Embracing Freedom and Moving Forward

The journey from shame to freedom is one of transformation, rooted in the unshakable truth of God's love and grace. By following the steps of acknowledging shame, repenting, speaking truth, and seeking a deeper relationship with God, we can break free from the power of shame and step into the fullness of life that God has prepared for us.

In Christ, we are no longer defined by our past, our failures, or the judgments of others. Instead, we are defined by His love, His sacrifice, and His promise of eternal life. As we embrace this truth, we can walk in the freedom and joy that comes from knowing we are forgiven, loved, and valued by the Creator of the universe.

Overcoming shame is a process that requires faith, courage, and a deep reliance on God's promises. By looking to the examples of biblical figures who have walked this path before us, we can find hope and encouragement to face our own battles with shame. Through Christ, we have the power to break free from shame's grip and live a life that reflects the glory of God's grace and redemption.

As we move forward, let us hold fast to the truth that in Christ, we are a new creation. The old has passed away, and the new has come (2 Corinthians 5:17). With this assurance, we can boldly step into the future, unburdened by shame, and fully embrace the life of purpose and joy that God has designed for us.

CHAPTER 09

Silencing the Accuser of Brethren

Silencing the Accuser of the Brethren
In the spiritual realm, two powerful forces are at work:
1. The Force of Satan - The "Accuser of the Brethren":
The name "Satan" is not just a label but a job description. It means "one who opposes or blocks." Imagine a basketball game where Satan plays a relentless defense, constantly trying to prevent you from making your best shot. He whispers discouraging thoughts like, "You can't do this!" or "You're not good enough!"

Beyond being an adversary, Satan also serves as "the accuser of our brothers and sisters" (Revelation 12:11, NLT). He acts like a prosecuting attorney, filing endless claims about our failures and why we are unworthy of God's use. These accusations form the core of the spiritual warfare we face, often hindering us from realizing our true destinies.

2. The Force of Jesus Christ - The Intercessor:

In contrast to Satan's accusations, Jesus Christ stands as our intercessor, pleading for our deliverance. Two examples of His intercessory spirit in action include:

- The Woman Caught in Adultery: Jesus said to her, "Where are your accusers? Go your way and sin no more."

- Zacchaeus and the Pharisee: Jesus dined with Zacchaeus, an unpopular tax collector, and intervened when the disciples wanted to call down fire from heaven as judgment.

The suffering Jesus endured on the cross was intended to heal our wounds, just as Isaiah prophesied: "By His wounds we were healed" (Isaiah 53:5). The cross is where our record of wrongs and shame was canceled, where Satan is dethroned and silenced in our lives (Colossians 2:14–15).

The Three Lies of the Accuser, Satan

Satan employs three primary lies to derail believers:

1. Lie 1: Doubt

Doubt is a strategy that Satan has used since the beginning of time. In the Garden of Eden, he tempted Eve by sowing seeds of doubt, questioning God's command, and implying that she could be like God. Eve should have responded, "I am already created in God's image." But instead, doubt led to a fall, and humanity has reaped the bitter consequences ever since. Many Christians are unaware of the lies Satan whispers, which not only accuse them but also distort their understanding of their relationship with God and their true identity.

2. Lie 2: Destiny

Satan tries to convince us that we will never reach our full potential or complete God's plan for our lives. He whispers that we will fall short of our destiny, aiming to discourage us from pursuing God's purpose.

3. Lie 3: Denunciation

Satan seeks to turn us into accusers rather than intercessors, urging us to criticize and condemn others. He wants us to impose shame on others, aligning us with his destructive agenda.

Dealing with the Lies of Satan

1. Overcoming Doubt:

The only sure way to overcome doubt is to place your faith in the Word of God.

2. Standing on God's Promise for Your Destiny:

Declare God's truth over your life: "For I know the thoughts that I think toward you, says the Lord, thoughts of peace and not of evil, to give you a future and a hope" (Jeremiah 29:11). Satan's lies are meant to silence us and prevent us from influencing others. He knows our testimonies can unleash the power of Jesus, so he tries to mute them with accusations. But through the blood of the Lamb and the power of our testimonies, we can take control of our pasts, silence Satan, and live victoriously.

3. Rejecting Denunciation:

Instead of condemning or accusing others, follow the guidance of God's Word: "Then I will teach transgressors Your ways, And sinners shall be converted to You" (Psalms 51:13).

Breaking the Force of Accusation in Your Life

To break free from the force of accusation, declare with confidence: "I will turn from the spirit of accusation to the spirit of intercession. I will reject doubt. I will say to the accuser, 'Get under my feet. You will not dominate my life. I will rise up to fulfill my destiny!' I will put my foot down on you and declare right now, 'I will be an intercessor.'"

When you feel the shame of Satan's accusations and guilt, don't succumb to them. Instead, pull out the enemy's fiery darts and throw them back! Refuse to believe his lies and boldly declare God's truth: "There is no condemnation for me because I am in Christ Jesus" (paraphrase of Romans 8:1).

Living in Victory Over the Accuser

Having recognized the tactics of Satan—the accuser—and armed ourselves with the truth of God's Word, the next step is to actively live in the victory that Christ has secured for us. This requires a daily commitment to reject the lies of the enemy, embrace our identity in Christ, and walk in the power of the Holy Spirit.

The Power of Our Testimony

One of the most effective weapons we have against the accuser is our testimony. Revelation 12:11 reminds us that "they overcame him by the blood of the Lamb and by the word of their testimony." Our testimony is not just our story; it is the evidence of God's work in our lives. When we share how God has transformed us, forgiven us, and set us free, we diminish the power of shame and silence the accuser.

Satan's goal is to keep us silent, to make us believe that our past disqualifies us from speaking out. But when we testify to God's grace, we declare that our identity is no longer defined by our past sins or the lies of the enemy. Instead, it is defined by who we are in Christ—redeemed, loved, and victorious.

Daily Strategies for Silencing the Accuser

1. Declare Your Identity in Christ:

Begin each day by affirming who you are in Christ. Speak scriptures that remind you of your righteousness, your worth, and your purpose. For example:

- "I am a new creation in Christ; the old has passed away, and the new has come" (2 Corinthians 5:17).

- "I am the righteousness of God in Christ Jesus" (2 Corinthians 5:21).

- "I can do all things through Christ who strengthens me" (Philippians 4:13).

2. Reject and Replace Lies with Truth:

Whenever a negative thought or accusation enters your mind, immediately recognize it as a lie from the enemy. Speak the truth of God's Word over yourself to counteract it. For example, if you hear the lie, "You are not good enough," respond with, "I am fearfully and wonderfully made" (Psalm 139:14).

3. Practice Forgiveness:

Just as Christ has forgiven us, we are called to forgive others. Holding onto bitterness or resentment gives the accuser a foothold in our lives. Choose to forgive those who have wronged you, and release any anger or hurt to God. This will not only free you but will also weaken the enemy's hold on you.

4. Engage in Spiritual Warfare:

Spiritual warfare is an ongoing battle, and prayer is one of our most powerful weapons. Ephesians 6:10-18 encourages us to put on the full armor of God so that we can stand against the schemes of the devil. Pray daily for protection, strength, and discernment. Use the authority you have in Christ to bind the enemy's attacks and declare victory over your life.

5. Surround Yourself with Godly Community:

Being part of a supportive, faith-filled community is crucial in standing firm against the accuser. Surround yourself with people who will encourage you, pray for you, and remind you of God's truth when you are struggling. Together, you can lift each other up and keep each other accountable in your walk with Christ.

6. Live Out Your Calling:

The accuser wants to derail you from fulfilling God's purpose for your life. Refuse to let fear or shame hold you back. Step out in faith, trusting that God will equip you for every good work He has prepared for you. Remember, "For we are His workmanship, created in Christ Jesus for good works, which God prepared beforehand, that we should walk in them" (Ephesians 2:10).

Walking in Freedom

As you commit to silencing the accuser and living in the truth of who you are in Christ, you will begin to experience greater freedom and victory in your life. The chains of shame, doubt, and fear will start to fall away as you grow in confidence in God's love and grace.

The more you embrace your identity in Christ, the less power the accuser will have over you. Your past will no longer define you, and the enemy's lies will no longer hold you captive. Instead, you will walk in the fullness of life that Jesus promised—a life of purpose, joy, and peace.

The battle against the accuser is real, but so is the victory that Christ has won for us. By standing firm in our faith, declaring God's truth, and living out our testimony, we can silence the accuser and live the abundant life that God has planned for us.

Remember, you are not fighting this battle alone. Jesus, our great intercessor, is standing with you, advocating for you, and empowering you through the Holy Spirit. As you continue to trust in Him, you will find that the accusations of the enemy grow quieter and the voice of God's truth becomes louder.

So, rise up in faith, silence the accuser, and walk boldly into the destiny that God has prepared for you!

CHAPTER 10

Life After Religion

Life After Religion

Finishing strong in life is not an easy task, and it doesn't happen overnight. It requires consistent effort, dedication to the calling God has given you, and finding joy in that work, making it as vital to you as your daily sustenance.

We often discuss how Jesus managed His time, worked diligently, prioritized wisely, and knew when to rest. But the central purpose of all His actions was to glorify God by completing the mission He was sent to accomplish—and doing so with excellence.

The Four Attributes of a Finisher

1. Acknowledge Jesus as Lord of Your Life:

The first step to becoming a finisher is to fully commit to God as the Lord of your life. This means humbling yourself before Him and allowing Him to change your heart, perspective, and priorities. It involves exchanging worldly desires for the riches of heaven and choosing a life in Christ over a life centered on earthly gains.

2. Associate Yourself with a Local Church:

Being part of a local church is crucial. In the fellowship of believers, where two or more are gathered in His name, Jesus is present to work miracles, provide comfort in times of crisis, and offer the support needed to stay on course.

3. Abandon Anxious Concerns:

Those with the spirit of a finisher do not sit idly in the rubble of negative circumstances. Instead, they cast all their concerns upon God. As Philippians 4:6-7 instructs, "Do not be anxious about anything, but in every situation, by prayer and petition, with thanksgiving, present your requests to God. And the peace of God, which transcends all understanding, will guard your hearts and your minds in Christ Jesus."

4. Adopt a Wartime Mentality:

Every day, put on the full armor of God to protect yourself from Satan's accusations and attacks (Ephesians 6:11-18). Lift your shield of faith to extinguish his fiery darts of shame. Stay alert and vigilant, as 1 Peter 5:8-9 warns, "Your enemy the devil prowls around like a roaring lion looking for someone to devour. Resist him, standing firm in the faith."

When we think of enduring to the end and finishing well, no one exemplifies this better than the Apostle Paul, aside from Jesus Himself. As Paul sat chained in a Roman prison, awaiting execution, he wrote to Timothy:

"For I am already being poured out as a drink offering, and the time of my departure has come. I have fought the good fight, I have finished the race, I have kept the faith. Henceforth there is laid up for me the crown of righteousness, which the Lord, the righteous judge, will award to me on that Day, and not only to me but also to all who have loved his appearing" (2 Timothy 4:6–8).

Steps to Strengthen Areas of Weakness

To improve any area of weakness, consider the following steps:

1. Identify the Weakness:

Start by honestly identifying the specific area that needs improvement, and seek feedback from others to gain clarity.

2. Set Specific Goals:

Once you've identified the weakness, set achievable and measurable goals to address it.

3. Create a Plan:

Develop a detailed plan of action that includes acquiring new skills, seeking support, and practicing specific behaviors to achieve your goals.

4. Take Action:

Implement your plan and take consistent steps towards improvement, exercising perseverance and patience along the way.

5. Seek Feedback:

Regularly seek feedback to monitor your progress and adjust your approach as necessary.

6. Celebrate Successes:

Celebrate your achievements, no matter how small, to stay motivated and engaged in the process of growth.

7. Reflect and Evaluate:

After reaching your goals, reflect on the progress made and evaluate your methods. Use this insight to identify new areas for improvement and continue building on your strengths.

Improving any area of weakness requires dedication, effort, and a willingness to learn and grow. By keeping your focus on God instead of the problem, praying over each situation, refusing to remain captive to shame, and taking these practical steps, you can overcome weaknesses and fulfill God's purpose for your life.

The Contrast Between David and Saul

David:

King David, despite his sins and the shame that followed, dealt with them head-on and went on to fulfill his God-given destiny. As Acts 13:36 states, "For David, after he had served his own generation by the will of God, fell asleep, was buried with his fathers..."

Saul:

King Saul, Israel's first king, struggled with pride and disobedience. He took matters into his own hands by offering a burnt sacrifice, which was against God's instructions. Unlike David, Saul did not finish well because he failed to stay aligned with God's plan.

To be strong finishers like Paul and David, we need to stay in sync with God's guidance every day. Think of it like using a GPS—God's Positioning System. Just as a GPS guides you through every turn, God's Word, the Bible, is our spiritual GPS. A wise person never starts their day or makes an important decision without consulting this divine guidance. After reading the Word, spend time in prayer, asking God for direction and your daily "marching orders," so you can make necessary corrections along the way.

Commitment to Finishing Well

As we age, the goal to finish well becomes even more significant. Whether you're in your 50s or your 90s, the commitment to continue working for God, studying, learning, and teaching remains vital. Following the example of Jesus and Paul, we should strive to finish the work we were sent to do and finish it with excellence. The journey is not over until the day we meet our Creator, and until then, we must continue to fight the good fight, keeping our eyes on the prize.

So, embrace the call to be a finisher. Use God's Word as your guide, stay focused on your mission, and trust that with His help, you will finish well.

The Importance of Perseverance in Finishing Well

Finishing well is not just about reaching the end; it's about how we journey through life with faith, commitment, and perseverance. Our ultimate goal is to complete the work that God has entrusted to us, and to do so with excellence, integrity, and a heart fully devoted to Him. This requires us to continually align ourselves with God's will, stay focused on our mission, and rely on His strength to overcome challenges along the way.

Examples of Finishing Well in the Bible

1. Paul's Journey of Perseverance:

The Apostle Paul is a profound example of someone who finished well despite facing immense trials and suffering. He endured beatings, imprisonment, shipwrecks, and persecution, yet he never wavered in his faith or his mission. Paul's life exemplifies unwavering commitment to God's calling, even in the face of death. His words to Timothy, written from a Roman prison, reflect his confidence in having fulfilled his divine assignment: "I have fought the good fight, I have finished the race, I have kept the faith" (2 Timothy 4:7).

2. Moses' Leadership to the End:

Moses, who led the Israelites out of Egypt and through the wilderness, also demonstrated what it means to finish well. Despite the challenges, frustrations, and personal shortcomings he faced, Moses remained faithful to God's calling until the end of his life. He didn't enter the Promised Land, but he completed the mission God gave him, leading His people to the brink of their inheritance. His life is a testament to the importance of obedience and steadfastness.

3. Jesus' Perfect Example:

Of course, the ultimate example of finishing well is Jesus Christ. His entire life was devoted to fulfilling the Father's will, culminating in His sacrifice on the cross. Jesus declared, "It is finished" (John 19:30), signifying the completion of the work of redemption. He perfectly carried out His mission, leaving us an example to follow. His life teaches us the importance of enduring hardships, remaining faithful to God's plan, and trusting in the ultimate victory that comes through Him.

Practical Steps to Finishing Well

1. Daily Dependence on God:

Finishing well requires daily reliance on God. This means starting each day with prayer, seeking His guidance, and aligning your plans with His will. It involves surrendering your struggles, anxieties, and ambitions to Him, trusting that He will provide the strength and wisdom you need to persevere.

2. Consistency in Spiritual Disciplines:

Cultivating a consistent spiritual routine is essential for staying strong in your faith. This includes regular prayer, Bible study, worship, and fellowship with other believers. These disciplines help you stay connected to God and grounded in His truth, enabling you to navigate life's challenges with grace and resilience.

3. Maintaining a Long-Term Perspective:

It's easy to get discouraged by the obstacles and setbacks we encounter along the way. However, maintaining a long-term perspective helps us stay focused on the bigger picture. Remember that your life is part of a larger story—God's story—and that every challenge you face is an opportunity to grow in faith and character. Keep your eyes on the eternal prize and press on with determination, knowing that your efforts will be rewarded.

4. Cultivating Relationships That Encourage Growth:

Surround yourself with people who will support you, challenge you, and hold you accountable. Seek out mentors, friends, and fellow believers who will encourage you to stay true to your calling and help you navigate difficult seasons. Healthy relationships provide the support and encouragement needed to finish well.

5. Continual Learning and Growth:

Never stop learning and growing, both spiritually and personally. Seek to develop your gifts, acquire new skills, and expand your understanding of God's Word. Staying engaged in the process of growth keeps you vibrant and effective in your ministry and life's work.

6. Serving Others with Humility:

Finishing well often involves pouring into others and leaving a legacy of faith. Serve others with humility, just as Jesus did, and invest in the next generation. By mentoring, teaching, and encouraging others, you can help them fulfill their own God-given purposes, ensuring that the impact of your life extends beyond your own time on earth.

The Final Reward

For those who finish well, there is a promise of eternal reward. Paul speaks of the "crown of righteousness" that awaits those who have faithfully run their race (2 Timothy 4:8). This crown is not just for Paul, but for all who love and long for Christ's appearance. The assurance of this reward gives us the motivation to endure, knowing that our labor is not in vain.

As you continue on your journey, remember that finishing well is not about perfection, but about perseverance. It's about staying the course, remaining faithful to God, and trusting Him to bring to completion the good work He has begun in you (Philippians 1:6). Whether you are in the early stages of your walk with God or nearing the end of your race, commit yourself to finishing well, so that when you stand before the Lord, you can hear the words, "Well done, good and faithful servant" (Matthew 25:21).

In the end, life after religion—life rooted in a deep relationship with God—is about more than just starting strong; it's about finishing strong. It's about living each day with purpose, determination, and a commitment to God's calling. As you strive to finish well, rely on the strength of the Holy Spirit, stay grounded in God's Word, and keep your eyes on the eternal prize. With God's help, you can finish the race with joy, knowing that you have faithfully fulfilled the work He set before you.

CHAPTER 11

Receiving Double for Your Shame

The prophet Jeremiah described the devastating effects of shame on Israel with these words: "For shame has devoured the labor of our fathers from our youth—their flocks and their herds, their sons and their daughters. We lie down in our shame, and our reproach covers us. For we have sinned against the Lord our God, we and our fathers, from our youth even to this day, and have not obeyed the voice of the Lord our God" (Jeremiah 3:24-25).

This shame was persistent and would not be lifted until the children of Israel sincerely repented and returned to the Lord. Unfortunately, the Israelites during Jeremiah's time were resistant to his message. They found his constant warnings of judgment irritating and refused to listen.

This scenario mirrors the world today, where believers who faithfully follow God's instructions are warning a lost and dying world of impending judgment (Revelation 3:10). Even though many are not heeding these warnings, we must persist in proclaiming the truth to save some from the inevitable judgment to come.

However, in Isaiah 61:7, the prophet brought a different message to God's people: "Instead of your shame you shall have double honor, and instead of confusion they shall rejoice in their portion. Therefore, in their land they shall possess double; Everlasting joy shall be theirs" (Isaiah 61:7).

Under the anointing of the Spirit and the ministry of the Messiah, a remarkable transformation was promised. Where there was once shame and dishonor, there would now be double honor. The concept of a double portion in the Bible typically refers to a double blessing, often associated with the birthright or inheritance given to the eldest son (Deuteronomy 21:17).

This promise extends to us as well. Jesus declared, "I have come that they may have life, and that they may have it more abundantly" (John 10:10). He came so that we might experience a superabundant life—a life filled with more than enough, a double portion. God is generous with His blessings, giving far beyond what we need. Anyone who lives in lack is not fully embracing the abundant life that Jesus offers.

Isaiah's promise is rooted in an Old Testament law that required double restitution for what an enemy stole (Exodus 22:4,7, and 9). This law underpins the concept of receiving double for your shame.

The Story of Elijah and Elisha: A Double Portion

In 2 Kings 2:1-14, we read about Elijah and Elisha, a powerful example of receiving a double portion. Elisha had a deep desire to minister with the same prophetic anointing as his master, Elijah. When Elijah was taken to heaven in a chariot of fire, his cloak—a symbol of God's anointing—fell upon Elisha. Elisha picked up the mantle and began his ministry with twice the power and impact that Elijah had.

Elisha's request for a double portion of Elijah's spirit was granted, and Scripture records that Elisha performed twice as many miracles (28) as Elijah (14). This is a clear example of receiving a double portion.

Another example is found in the life of Job. After his time of intense testing, God restored to Job twice as much as he had before: "And the Lord restored the fortunes of Job when he had prayed for his friends. And the Lord gave Job twice as much as he had before" (Job 42:10). Job, too, received a "double portion."

Applying These Lessons to Your Life

How can these examples be applied to your life? By recognizing that true power and blessing come from God, not from seeking reputation or position. Understanding that God is with you enables you to deliver His message boldly, without fear of the enemy's accusations or shame.

While we all desire God's blessings, they are not automatically granted. We must diligently seek them. The Bible clearly teaches that God is eager to pour out His blessings on His people, but only when we align our lives with His will and seek Him as our greatest blessing and first priority.

Helping Others Overcome Shame

The truths you've learned from this book can be powerful tools to help others who are restrained or bound by shame. By sharing these insights, you can encourage them to seek God's blessing, embrace the abundant life He offers, and live free from the shame that once held them back. Through your guidance, they can experience the double portion of honor and joy that God promises to those who trust in Him.

Moving Forward with God's Promise of Abundance

Having understood the significance of receiving double for your shame and how God's promises of restoration and abundance apply to your life, the next step is to actively live in this truth and help others do the same. The journey from shame to honor is not just about personal restoration but also about becoming a vessel through which God's grace and truth can flow to others.

Embracing Your Double Portion

Living in the reality of God's promise means embracing the double portion of His blessings in every area of your life. This includes:

1. Walking in Faith:

Trust in God's promise to restore and bless you beyond what you've lost or endured. Like Elisha, who boldly asked for a double portion of Elijah's spirit, approach God with confidence, knowing that He is willing and able to bless you abundantly. This requires faith, not only in God's power but also in His desire to see you thrive and flourish.

2. Living Abundantly:

Jesus came to give us life more abundantly. This abundant life isn't just about material wealth but encompasses spiritual richness, emotional well-being, and the fulfillment of God's purpose in your life. Embrace the fullness of what God has for you, refusing to settle for less than what He has promised.

3. Proclaiming Your Freedom:

As you walk in the freedom that comes from receiving God's double portion, proclaim this freedom to others. Share your testimony of how God has transformed your shame into honor and how He can do the same for them. Your story can be a powerful tool in helping others break free from the chains of shame and step into their own double portion.

4. Seeking God First:

To fully experience the double portion, make seeking God your highest priority. As you align your life with His will and pursue a deeper relationship with Him, you'll find that His blessings naturally flow into your life. The more you seek God Himself, rather than just His blessings, the more you'll discover the true richness of life in Him.

Helping Others Experience Double for Their Shame

One of the most rewarding aspects of walking in God's promise is the opportunity to help others experience the same transformation. Here's how you can apply the truths you've learned to support those who are struggling with shame:

1. Offer Compassion and Understanding:

People bound by shame often feel isolated and misunderstood. Offer them compassion and a listening ear. Sometimes, simply being present and empathetic can open the door for them to begin healing.

2. Share Biblical Truths:

Use the scriptures and stories you've learned to encourage others. Share how God's promise of a double portion applies to their situation, and help them see that their shame does not have to define them. Remind them of God's faithfulness in restoring those who turn to Him.

3. Encourage Repentance and Restoration:

Just as the Israelites needed to repent and return to God to experience restoration, guide others to recognize the need for repentance in their own lives. Help them understand that true restoration begins with turning back to God and seeking His forgiveness.

4. Walk with Them in Faith:

Help others build their faith by walking with them through their journey. Pray with them, encourage them to trust in God's promises, and celebrate with them as they begin to see God's restoration in their lives.

5. Be a Role Model of Hope:

Your life can be a beacon of hope for those who are struggling. As you live out the principles of receiving double for your shame, others will see the tangible evidence of God's work in your life. This can inspire them to believe that God can do the same for them.

Living Out the Promise

The journey of receiving double for your shame is ongoing. As you continue to seek God and walk in His promises, remember that the process involves growth, learning, and continual reliance on His grace. There may be challenges along the way, but the promise of a double portion is one of hope and assurance that God's plans for you are for good and not for harm (Jeremiah 29:11).

God's promise to give you double for your shame is a powerful testimony of His grace and restorative power. It is an invitation to rise above the shame of the past and step into a future filled with honor, joy, and abundance. By embracing this promise in your own life and sharing it with others, you can be a conduit of God's blessing, helping others to break free from shame and live in the fullness of life that God offers.

As you move forward, continue to seek God's guidance, trust in His promises, and live out the abundant life He has planned for you. Remember, the God who restored Job, who gave Elisha a double portion, and who promised Israel double honor for their shame, is the same God who is ready to pour out His blessings on you. Step into your double portion and live with the confidence that God is with you, ready to give you more than you can ask or imagine.

Shalom,

Dr. Maxwell Shimba

OVERCOMING SHAME

Conclusion: Embracing a Life Free from Shame

As we reach the conclusion of this journey, it's essential to reflect on the powerful transformation that overcoming shame can bring to your life. Throughout this book, we've explored the deep and often hidden impact of shame on our hearts, minds, and relationships. But more importantly, we've delved into the path toward freedom—how to acknowledge, confront, and ultimately release the shame that has held us back.

Overcoming shame is not just about letting go of past hurts; it's about stepping into a new identity rooted in truth, grace, and the unshakable love of God. It's about understanding that you are not defined by your mistakes, your past, or the lies that have been spoken over you. Instead, you are defined by the One who created you, who sees you as worthy, valuable, and beloved.

As you continue to apply the principles and truths you've learned, you will find yourself increasingly free to live the life you were meant to live—a life of purpose, joy, and connection. You'll begin to experience the profound benefits of overcoming shame, including enhanced self-esteem, stronger relationships, greater resilience, and a deeper sense of self-awareness and freedom.

But the journey doesn't end here. The freedom from shame is an ongoing process, one that requires daily commitment, faith, and reliance on God's grace. As you move forward, continue to seek God's presence, lean on His strength, and trust in His promises. Allow His love to reshape your identity, your relationships, and your future.

In the end, overcoming shame is about reclaiming your God-given identity and walking in the fullness of life that Jesus came to give. It's about living each day with the confidence that you are free, forgiven, and fully accepted by the One who knows you best and loves you most.

So, take the next step. Embrace the freedom that awaits you. Live boldly, love deeply, and let your life be a testament to the transformative power of God's grace and truth. Your journey of healing and growth is just beginning, and with God by your side, the possibilities are limitless.

APPENDICES

Appendix A: Key Scriptures on Overcoming Shame

1. Isaiah 61:7

"Instead of your shame you shall have double honor, and instead of confusion they shall rejoice in their portion. Therefore in their land they shall possess double; everlasting joy shall be theirs."

2. Romans 8:1

"There is therefore now no condemnation for those who are in Christ Jesus."

3. Psalm 34:4-5

"I sought the Lord, and He answered me and delivered me from all my fears. Those who look to Him are radiant, and their faces shall never be ashamed."

4. 1 John 1:9

"If we confess our sins, He is faithful and just to forgive us our sins and to cleanse us from all unrighteousness."

5. Joel 2:26

"You shall eat in plenty and be satisfied, and praise the name of the Lord your God, who has dealt wondrously with you; and my people shall never again be put to shame."

Appendix B: Practical Steps to Overcoming Shame

1. Acknowledge the Shame:

Recognize and admit the shame you are experiencing. Denial only prolongs its hold on you.

2. Seek God's Forgiveness and Grace:

Bring your shame to God in prayer. Confess any sin and ask for His forgiveness, knowing that He is faithful to cleanse you from all unrighteousness.

3. Renew Your Mind with God's Word:

Replace the lies of shame with the truth of God's Word. Meditate on scriptures that speak of your identity in Christ and His love for you.

4. Surround Yourself with Supportive Community:

Engage with a faith-based community that can provide encouragement, accountability, and support as you work through your shame.

5. Focus on Your Identity in Christ:

Continuously remind yourself that your identity is in Christ, not in your past mistakes or the shame that once bound you.

6. Serve Others:

Sometimes, stepping out of your own struggles and helping others can provide perspective and healing. Serving allows you to see beyond your own challenges and experience the joy of giving.

Appendix C: Resources for Further Study and Support

1. Books:

- "The Wounded Heart" by Dan Allender: A book on healing from abuse and overcoming shame.

- "Shame Interrupted" by Edward T. Welch: This book explores how God lifts the burden of shame.

2. Support Groups:

- Celebrate Recovery: A Christ-centered program that helps people overcome hurts, habits, and hang-ups, including shame.

- GriefShare: A support group for those dealing with the loss and the shame that can accompany it.

3. Counseling:

- Christian Counseling & Educational Foundation (CCEF): Provides biblical counseling and resources.

- Focus on the Family Counseling Services: Offers referrals to licensed Christian counselors.

Appendix D: Journaling Prompts for Reflection and Healing

1. Identifying Shame:

Reflect on moments in your life where you have felt shame. What triggered these feelings? How have they impacted your actions and self-perception?

2. Scripture Meditation:

Choose a scripture that speaks to overcoming shame and meditate on it. Write down your thoughts and how it applies to your life.

3. Forgiveness and Release:

Who do you need to forgive, including yourself? Write a letter of forgiveness, even if you never send it, as a way to release the burden of shame.

4. God's Perspective:

Reflect on how God sees you, according to His Word. Write down affirmations based on your identity in Christ.

5. Vision for the Future:

Imagine a life free from shame. What does it look like? How would you act differently? Write down your vision and steps you can take to move toward it.

Appendix E: Prayers for Overcoming Shame

1. A Prayer for Healing from Shame:

"Heavenly Father, I come before You, burdened by shame. I ask for Your healing touch to cleanse me from all unrighteousness. Help me to see myself as You see me—loved, valued, and forgiven. I lay my shame at Your feet and ask for Your grace to fill my heart. Restore to me the joy of Your salvation and help me walk in the freedom You have given me. In Jesus' name, Amen."

2. A Prayer for Strength and Resilience:

"Lord, when I am tempted to give in to shame, remind me of Your truth. Strengthen me to stand firm in my identity in You. Help me to resist the lies of the enemy and to walk boldly in the path You have set before me. Give me resilience in the face of adversity and courage to pursue the life You have called me to live. In Jesus' name, Amen."

3. A Prayer for a New Beginning:

"Father God, I thank You for the new beginning You offer through Christ. I release the past and embrace the new life You have given me. Help me to live each day in the light of Your love, free from the shadows of shame. Guide me as I walk in Your purpose and help me to reflect Your glory in all that I do. In Jesus' name, Amen."

These appendices are designed to provide you with practical tools, resources, and spiritual support as you continue your journey toward healing and freedom from shame. May they serve as a guide to help you walk in the fullness of life that God has prepared for you.

THEOLOGICAL QUESTIONS

Theological questions for each chapter of your book:

Introduction

1. What role does shame play in the human experience according to Christian theology?

2. How has the concept of shame evolved throughout biblical history?

3. What is the significance of addressing shame from a theological perspective?

Chapter 01: What is Shame According to the Bible?

1. How does the Bible define shame, and how does it differ from guilt?

2. What are the first instances of shame mentioned in the Bible, and what can we learn from them?

3. How does the concept of shame in the Bible relate to the idea of sin and separation from God?

Chapter 02: The Generational Shame

1. How does the Bible address the concept of generational sin and shame?

2. What biblical examples illustrate the transmission of shame from one generation to another?

3. How can generational shame be broken according to biblical principles?

Chapter 03: Inherited Shame

1. What does the Bible say about inherited sin and its connection to shame?

2. How does the doctrine of original sin relate to the concept of inherited shame?

3. In what ways does Christ's redemptive work address and heal inherited shame?

Chapter 04: Individual Shame

1. How does the Bible differentiate between individual shame and collective shame?

2. What biblical characters experienced individual shame, and how did they overcome it?

3. How can Christians apply biblical teachings to overcome personal shame in their lives?

Chapter 05: Incessant Shame

1. What are the biblical roots of incessant shame, and how does it manifest in a believer's life?

2. How does incessant shame hinder spiritual growth, according to biblical teachings?

3. What biblical strategies can be employed to break the cycle of incessant shame?

Chapter 06: Imposed Shame

1. How does the Bible address shame that is imposed by others, such as through societal or relational pressures?

2. What examples from Scripture illustrate how imposed shame was dealt with or overcome?

3. How should Christians respond to imposed shame in light of biblical teachings?

Chapter 07: Institutional Shame

1. What does the Bible say about shame that arises from institutional or systemic sin?

2. How can believers work to rectify institutional shame within their communities and organizations?

3. What lessons can be learned from biblical stories where institutional shame was present and addressed?

Chapter 08: Shattering The Obstacles

1. What obstacles to overcoming shame are mentioned in the Bible, and how can they be shattered?

2. How does faith in Christ empower believers to break free from the obstacles of shame?

3. What role does the Holy Spirit play in helping believers overcome shame-related obstacles?

Chapter 09: Silencing the Accuser of Brethren

1. What is the role of Satan as the accuser in the context of shame, according to the Bible?

2. How does the Bible instruct believers to combat the accusations of Satan and overcome shame?

3. What biblical promises can Christians rely on to silence the voice of the accuser?

Chapter 10: Life After Religion

1. How does the Bible describe life in Christ as opposed to life bound by religious shame?

2. What does the transition from religion to a relationship with Christ look like in overcoming shame?

3. How can believers experience the fullness of life that Jesus promised after overcoming shame?

Chapter 11: Receiving Double for Your Shame

1. What does the Bible mean by receiving "double for your shame," and where is this concept found?

2. How does God's promise of restoration apply to those who have been burdened by shame?

3. What role does faith play in claiming God's promise of receiving double for your shame?

Overcoming Shame (Conclusion)

1. How does the Bible provide a framework for overcoming shame in various aspects of life?

2. What practical steps, based on Scripture, can believers take to fully overcome shame?

3. How can the process of overcoming shame lead to a deeper understanding and relationship with God?

These questions are designed to provoke thought and discussion, helping readers to deepen their understanding of shame from a biblical perspective and apply these insights to their personal lives.